"One of the most important lessons from the New Testament is that gospel churches naturally cooperate in gospel ministries. That's why I welcome this new book by Chris Bruno and Matt Dirks. The rising generation of young evangelicals needs to embrace once again a fully biblical understanding of cooperation so churches united in faith can cooperate together to share the gospel with the world."

> **R. Albert Mohler, Jr.,** President and Joseph Emerson Brown Professor of Christian Theology, The Southern Baptist Theological Seminary

"God's mission is too big for any one church to accomplish. We know that. Yet we often act as if our church must do it all—alone. How freeing to discover what can happen when churches join forces. Chris Bruno and Matt Dirks are scholars with pastors' hearts, and they tackle the topic with theological depth and practical wisdom. Their strategies for kingdom partnerships will leave readers inspired to seek out partner congregations and well equipped to make the partnerships flourish. For church leaders more excited about building God's kingdom than their own, this is the book to read."

> **Drew Dyck,** Managing Editor, *Leadership Journal*; author, *Yawning at Tigers: You Can't Tame God, So Stop Trying*

"The world has become too complex and challenging, and gospel opportunities too numerous, for Christ's followers to work in isolation from one another, much less compete with each other. The twenty-first century must be a century of partnerships; as long as the Lord tarries, we need to work together to advance the gospel. That's why I'm delighted to commend this thoroughly biblical and eminently practical book."

> **Todd A. Wilson,** Senior Pastor, Calvary Memorial Church, Oak Park, Illinois

"God can and does work miracles through local churches linked together by the gospel for the sake of loving their communities by introducing them to Jesus. I love the vision Chris and Matt live out and lay out in this book. May their tribe increase!"

> **Collin Hansen,** Editorial Director, The Gospel Coalition; author, *Young, Restless, Reformed: A Journalist's Journey with the New Calvinists*

"Unfortunately, smaller churches are too often deemed to be less faithful or significant. Bruno and Dirks cast a biblical vision for how such churches can partner together, providing a biblical foundation and practical strategies for such endeavors. The book makes a fresh and important contribution, and should be read widely."

Thomas R. Schreiner, James Buchanan Harrison Professor of New Testament Interpretation, The Southern Baptist Theological Seminary

"When gospel renewal grips our communities, it will be the fruit of churches collaborating in kingdom partnerships. *Churches Partnering Together* provides the requisite instruction and inspiration to make this vision a reality."

Chris Castaldo, Director, Ministry of Gospel Renewal, Billy Graham Center; author, *Talking to Catholics About Faith*

"Gospel partnership, rightly understood, always extends beyond individuals to churches. This book is an outstanding resource. It lays out, compellingly, the biblical rationale for churches partnering together with the aim of gospel advance. It is full of useful examples and practical advice about partnership in action. I recommend it wholeheartedly."

William Taylor, Rector, St. Helen's Church, Bishopgate; author, *Understanding the Times* and *Partnership*

"Having recently begun to benefit from this very kind of relationship with four other local churches, I find myself very excited about *Churches Partnering Together*. I trust God will use this book to expose many more to the beauty and strength of these partnerships of mutual encouragement, shared resources, and shared labor. The work that Jesus has called his church to do will be greatly empowered as more of us follow the course that Chris and Matt lay out here. They give us not just a compelling vision but also the practicalities of pursuing these partnerships, with due attention to important things such as a solid relational foundation and prayer."

Mike Bullmore, Senior Pastor, Crossway Community Church, Bristol, Wisconsin

"Can even small congregations play a large part in the Great Commission? This book answers the question with a resounding yes—as they develop kingdom partnerships where they don't own anything, control anything, or count anything as their own. If you want to make a difference in the expansion of the gospel, read this book! It provides simple advice that can yield profound results."

William J. Hamel, President, Evangelical Free Church of America

"Partnerships make the most important things in life happen. What none of us can do alone can often be done in collaboration with others. Many pastors and church planters will benefit enormously from the wisdom, biblical insight, and practical experience that Chris Bruno and Matt Dirks provide for us here. May God be pleased to spread the vision, and share the work, for the growth of kingdom churches that advance the gospel of Christ."

Bruce A. Ware, Professor of Christian Theology, The Southern Baptist Theological Seminary

"Chris and Matt illustrate the power and multiplication factor of partnerships to see the kingdom of God expand. Out of their own experiences, they provide a road map for congregations of any size to partner together with others for powerful results. They write with kingdom hearts and gospel-centered focus. I highly recommend this book to any who are involved in the Great Commission."

T. J. Addington, Senior Vice President, Evangelical Free Church of America; Leader, ReachGlobal; author, *High-Impact Church Boards* and *Leading from the Sandbox*

"Ever since the apostle Paul thanked the church at Philippi for their partnership in the gospel, churches with a vision bigger than themselves have joined together to establish kingdom partnerships. Chris Bruno and Matt Dirks help us to see how local fellowships willing to walk humbly and depend together on the power of God can become catalysts for gospel-centered outreach to their communities and to the nations. How might we multiply the seed God has entrusted to us and extend the reign of Christ with one another to the glory of God? You will be both challenged and encouraged as you read this strong exhortation to kingdom building through church partnerships."

Bill Mills, Founder, Leadership Resources International

CHURCHES PARTNERING TOGETHER

Biblical Strategies for Fellowship, Evangelism, and Compassion

CHRIS BRUNO AND MATT DIRKS

::: CROSSWAY

WHEATON, ILLINOIS

Churches Partnering Together: Biblical Strategies for Fellowship, Evangelism, and Compassion

Copyright © 2014 by Christopher R. Bruno and Matthew D. Dirks

Published by Crossway
   1300 Crescent Street
   Wheaton, Illinois 60187

Cover design: Keane Fine

First printing 2014

Printed in the United States of America

Trade paperback ISBN: 978-1-4335- 4126-1
ePub ISBN: 978-1-4335-4129-2
PDF ISBN: 978-1-4335-4127-8
Mobipocket ISBN: 978-1-4335-4128-5

Library of Congress Cataloging-in-Publication Data

Bruno, Chris, 1980–
 Churches partnering together : biblical strategies for fellowship, evangelism, and compassion / Chris Bruno and Matt Dirks.
   pages cm
 Includes bibliographical references and index.
 ISBN 978-1-4335-4126-1 (tp)
 1. Church—Unity. 2. Interdenominational cooperation.
I. Title.
BV601.5.B78   2014
280'.042—dc23   2013044701

To our Lord,
our wives,
and our kids

They have all given us
much more grace
than we deserve

Contents

Foreword

If you are part of a big church, this book probably won't interest you.

But countless tens of thousands of us belong to small churches. Many of these churches are very small—so small it is difficult for one of them to imagine, at the moment, planting another church, fully supporting an overseas missionary, or several other things that need resources beyond the capacity of one small church.

Sometimes the challenge is reasonably well met within the framework of denominational structures: small churches with a common heritage and vision working together. Sometimes, however (let us be frank), churches within our own denominations do not share our understanding of and passion for the gospel of Jesus Christ. We may then find deeper gospel-based links across denominational lines. That, too, is happening.

In England, these movements are called gospel partnerships—Free Churches and Church of England congregations, often fairly small, are working together to train workers and plant churches, remaining not too concerned about the denominational outcome provided the gospel is joyously and faithfully upheld. Likewise, in the United States, some churches that align themselves with the Gospel Coalition are developing similar patterns in certain regions. The book you are holding tells of the outworking of one such partnership in one such region—Hawaii.

One does not have to agree with every pastoral decision adopted by Chris Bruno and Matt Dirks to realize that these brothers have important things to say, an important vision to cast, and important experiences to share with those of us who are members of small churches.

D. A. Carson
Research Professor of New Testament
Trinity Evangelical Divinity School

Acknowledgments

No book is written in isolation, especially not a book about partnership. We're extremely grateful to the many people who were involved in the process of research and writing.

Don Carson gave us some very helpful input in the early stages of mapping out our research, then contributed the foreword. Kevin DeYoung and Tom Schreiner interacted with us about the kingdom of God, and Michael Haykin saved us hours of research by providing help on some early church history. Pete Cavanagh helped us think through a biblical theology of partnership. Andy Krause, Ellen Livingood, George Stagg, Matthew Spandler-Davidson, Jay Jarman, Alan Nagel, Dan Chittock, and Justin Anderson shared their own partnership experiences. David Griffiths, Gary Summers, Todd Morikawa, and Andy Krause provided us with invaluable feedback on the manuscript. Our heartfelt thanks to you all.

It's not uncommon to hear authors rave about their positive experience working with Crossway, and it has been a joy for us to partner with a publisher that is truly committed to producing books that bring glory to God and advance the gospel. Dave DeWit and Greg Bailey deserve special thanks for their wisdom, guidance, and patience along the way.

We are also grateful to the leaders and people of Harbor Church, who have made this book and our church partnerships possible. Our fellow elders Ethan Pien, Justin Geer, and John Boehm have continually sought God's kingdom first. Our partner churches and pastors in the Gospel Coalition Hawaii, Antioch School Hawaii, EFCA Hawaii, and Acts 29 model kingdom generosity as they so often joyfully defer their own desires in order to bless others. Brad Barshaw, the senior pastor of the church that planted ours along with two others, has always displayed a radically sacrificial desire to build God's kingdom rather than his own castle.

We're so thankful for our amazing wives and kids, who consistently showed us love, joy, peace, patience, kindness, goodness, faithfulness, gentleness, and self-control (as much as a three-year-old can) as we worked on this book. Matt's wife, Cyndi, and his kids Caleb, Talia, Micah, and Kaira, and Chris's wife, Katie, and his sons Luke, Simon, and Elliot have supported us in every way possible.

Finally, we praise God for continually pouring out his undeserved grace on us both. The Father, Son, and Holy Spirit have ministered to us in many unexpected ways as we have written this book. Our passionate prayer is that he might be glorified as churches come together to advance his kingdom.

Introduction

What's your goal for the next ten years?

We're not talking about losing twenty pounds or learning to speak Chinese. We're talking about the one thing you would spend years of your life to accomplish. What would you travel across oceans and continents to achieve? What would you give your very life for?

Once you have that in mind, think about how the apostle Paul would have answered that question as he was just starting out in ministry. Would his goal have been one hundred baptisms a year? A church planted in every major city in the Roman empire? The conversion of Caesar?

You might be surprised to find out what Paul actually spent the most time, energy, and relational capital pursuing during his first decade of ministry: he worked to build a partnership of Gentile churches to support the struggling Jewish Christians in Jerusalem.

We know—we were surprised too. But one scholar said it best after surveying the New Testament evidence: "It is hard to imagine any campaign more embracing of the northern Mediterranean and any project that occupied Paul's attention more than this collection for the saints."[1]

---

[1] Scot McKnight, "Collection for the Saints," in *Dictionary of Paul and His Letters*, ed. Gerald F. Hawthorne, Ralph P. Martin, and Daniel G. Reid (Downers Grove, IL: InterVarsity, 1993), 143.

In fact, the Jerusalem collection partnership seems to pop up everywhere in the New Testament. We just don't pay much attention to it.

Every Easter, we revel in Paul's resurrection victory chant: "'Death is swallowed up in victory.' 'O death, where is your victory? O death, where is your sting?'" (1 Cor. 15:54b–55). We want to live out Paul's implications of the resurrection: "Be steadfast, immovable, always abounding in the work of the Lord, knowing that in the Lord your labor is not in vain" (v. 58). But then we ignore Paul's specific application of *labor* in the very next verse: "Concerning the *collection for the saints*: as I directed the churches of Galatia, so you also are to do" (16:1).

You can find many more references to the collection in Paul's letters and in Acts. He just couldn't stop talking about it. And by the time Paul finally delivered the gift to Jerusalem, he was bringing money and representatives from almost every region where he had planted churches.[2] This was a multinational church partnership that Paul viewed as the "seal" and "fruit" of his entire ministry![3] And you might be surprised to find out what kind of churches led it.

Big and Small

Many people assume that only big churches and parachurch ministries can accomplish big things. True, since the day of Pentecost, God has used large churches for some incredible achievements.

---

[2] "He had the following funds and/or people representing his missionary efforts: from the Galatian region (1 Cor 16:1) we hear of Derbe (Acts 20:4) and Lystra (Acts 20:4); from Macedonia (2 Cor 8:1–5; 9:2, 4) we hear of Berea (Acts 20:4), Thessalonica (20:4) and Philippi (cf. Acts 16:16 and 20:6; an inference about the "we" sections of Acts . . .); from Achaia we hear of Corinth (Rom 15:26; 1 Cor 16:1–4); from Mysia and Lydia we hear of Ephesus (Acts 20:4) and perhaps Troas (Acts 20:5–6); it is possible that funds came from Tyre (Acts 21:3–4), Ptolemais (Acts 21:7), and from both Cyprus and Caesarea (Acts 21:16). It is even possible that funds were collected from Rome (cf. Rom 12:13; 15:26 with 2 Cor 8:4; 9:13; and Rom 1:13 with 2 Cor 9:6–10)." (McKnight, "Collection for the Saints," 143–44.)

[3] This is how he describes it in the original Greek in Romans 15:28.

In the first century, the three thousand-plus-member Jerusalem church developed a widespread ministry to the needy, resulting in daily conversions among the same people who had just crucified Jesus. In the nineteenth century, the Metropolitan Tabernacle in London founded a pastors' college, an orphanage, and a Christian literature society, and even helped launch Hudson Taylor's China Inland Mission. In the twenty-first century, Redeemer Presbyterian Church in New York City has launched more than one hundred churches in the New York metro area, led a church-planting movement on six continents, and become one of the most influential voices on faith and religion in Manhattan. God has used large churches such as these to advance the kingdom powerfully across cities, regions, and the world.

But most churches are not large churches. The majority of congregations in the United States have fewer than seventy-five people. In our beloved home of Hawaii, as in many parts of the world, most are smaller than forty. These churches barely have enough money to support a pastor and pay the upkeep on a building or the rent for a school cafeteria. How can they make an impact beyond their church walls? They have a heartfelt desire to contribute to kingdom-advancing causes in missions, compassion, and leadership development, but many conclude that their only option is to send their money and people away to another organization to fulfill it.

However, the first-century churches in Macedonia, Achaia, and Asia Minor point us in another direction. It's crucial to understand that the most significant ministry effort of the first century wasn't a parachurch ministry or a megachurch ministry. The Jerusalem collection was spearheaded and sustained by small congregations. We would call them *kingdom churches*.

Kingdom Churches

Kingdom churches, whether they are large or small, are churches that want to build the kingdom, not just their own castles; that joyfully defer their own desires in order to bless others; and that eagerly partner with other congregations, setting aside second-ary theological and philosophical differences as they unite in the gospel.

In this book, we will explore how churches, big and small, can partner together for the sake of the kingdom. We want to help smaller-church leaders see possibilities for kingdom impact they might not have envisioned before, and we want to help bigger-church leaders see the blessing of working alongside smaller churches. We will encourage smaller churches to stop passively coveting megachurches and larger churches to stop trying to go it alone. Instead, we will urge large and small churches to start dreaming big dreams for the kingdom *together*. We'll also give lots of practical guidance from our own expe-rience and the experience of others that will help bring these dreams to reality.

Kingdom Partnerships

Here's the definition that will form the foundation for the rest of the book:

> A kingdom partnership is a gospel-driven relationship between interdependent local churches that pray, work, and share resources together strategically to glorify God through kingdom-advancing goals they could not accomplish alone.[4]

We'll explore different facets of that definition much more in the following chapters, but there are a few things we want to emphasize now. First, a kingdom partnership is *gospel-driven*. The gospel of God's glory and grace must be both the fuel and

---

[4]For the basis of this definition, we are indebted to ReachGlobal staff (Andy Krause, Roger Dorris, and Mark Morgenstern), who have done much thinking and practical work toward building missions partnerships between churches and organizations in the West and those in the majority world (http://go.efca.org/resources/document/reachglobal-partnerships).

final goal of any effective kingdom partnership. This foundation keeps it from becoming like so many once-vibrant ministries that began to assume the gospel, then ignore the gospel, and are now doing many good humanitarian things but have no real kingdom impact. Second, it is *interdependent*. It's not just a way for bigger, wealthier churches to feel better about themselves by helping smaller, poorer churches. Every church can expect to gain something from the others in such a partnership. Third, it is *God-glorifying*. When the world sees diverse churches working humbly and joyfully together, many people are led to give glory to the Father in heaven.

In our little corner of the globe, we have seen churches of many sizes that, inspired by the example of the churches of the New Testament, partner across denominational lines to plan seminars and conferences together, bring the gospel to dangerous places together, do overseas ministry together, and even train and support pastors and church planters together. God is working in powerful ways to expand his kingdom through these partnerships. But Hawaii isn't the only place this is happening. We're hearing similar stories from kingdom partnerships around the world.

What Partnership Is Not

But before we go too much further exploring what a kingdom partnership is, it's important to understand what it's *not*. In our experience, there are some temptations that every partnership starts to slide toward. These are things we must continually resist:

1. *A kingdom partnership is not a lowest-common-denominator ecumenical fellowship*. No church should compromise its gospel integrity for the sake of a partnership. Sadly, many mainline Protestant denominations have fallen victim to this temptation. As liberalism encroached in the early twentieth century, denominations chose unity

at all costs, and the result was a disaster. If we are serious about advancing the gospel in our partnerships, it's crucial to hold the essentials of the faith with a closed hand.

2. *A kingdom partnership is not a parachurch organization.* We might be stepping on some toes here, but we believe that many parachurch organizations have wrongfully usurped the role God gave to the local church. Most of these Christian organizations were established with the commendable desire to step in for churches that were failing to minister effectively to youth, college students, unreached people groups, and such, but they took this ministry away from the church rather than coming alongside the church to help her fulfill her God-given mission. A kingdom partnership is careful to avoid this temptation. Its goal is to facilitate and enhance the ministry of local churches, not replace them (for a simple explanation of the differences between local churches, parachurch organizations, and kingdom partnerships, see the appendix at the end of the book).

3. *A kingdom partnership is not a way for pastors to escape draining ministry in their local churches.* This is a big temptation for some pastors. Long-term ministry in a local church is exhausting! There's always another couple to counsel (again), another young man struggling with lust (again), and another boring administrative meeting to attend (again). Many pastors are tempted to neglect the shepherding responsibilities God has called them to carry out in their own churches so they can spend more time pursuing exciting ministry opportunities outside. But a true kingdom partnership fits into and even enhances the shepherding and equipping we do in our own churches.

4. *A kingdom partnership is not simply a pastors' fellowship.* While many fruitful partnerships are birthed out of relationships pastors have already established with one

another, the goal of a kingdom partnership is to get many different parts of the body involved. In a partnership to care for abused women, some members of each church do frontline outreach, other people provide short-term housing, a few do crisis counseling, others do long-term discipleship, and many more donate money, clothes, toiletries, and toys. Through widespread involvement, each local church is more unified and the partnership is more effective. The community is blessed and the kingdom is expanded.

What's Ahead

There are three movements in this book:

1. *The biblical/theological basis for a kingdom partnership.* In the first few chapters, we'll investigate how and why first-century churches worked together for kingdom-advancing goals. We experienced many surprises when we dug into the way these early church partnerships worked.
2. *The process of launching a partnership.* In the middle section, we'll see what it takes to get churches working together in a healthy way. A fruitful partnership doesn't just sprout up on its own. It takes an intentional process of building trust, determining God's call, developing goals and strategies, leveraging influence, and deploying resources well.
3. *The goal of expanding and multiplying a partnership.* It's often easier to start something than to maintain and grow it, so in the last section we'll discover how we can keep momentum going in a partnership, and how we can see God expand it beyond what we asked or imagined. We'll explore what it takes to turn a ministry into a movement!

Almost every sentence in the book was written collaboratively by Chris and Matt, but we use the pronoun *I* when Matt is speaking personally and the name *Chris* when Chris is speaking personally.

Our deeply heartfelt prayer is that God would use this book to assist you and your church in your quest to glorify him by working together with like-minded leaders and churches to advance his kingdom.

1

Catching the Vision

Understanding Kingdom Partnership

> *I thank my God in all my remembrance of you, always in every prayer of mine for you all making my prayer with joy, because of your partnership in the gospel from the first day until now.*
>
> PHILIPPIANS 1:3–5

There are a hundred reasons why you shouldn't work together with other churches.

You have limited time, resources, and people in your church. Isn't it possible to overcommit these God-given gifts by deploying them in ways God doesn't intend? Your church has a unique theological and philosophical identity. What if you wake up and find yourself unequally yoked to another church that believes and behaves differently? You have a deep desire to reach people and influence them to see God the way you see him. Won't there be people who are reached by your partnership ministry who decide to go to other churches or denominations? After all, you're only half-joking when you call other churches "the competition."

So why do it? What would drive churches, already stretched thin by their own ministry needs and financial pressures, to engage in kingdom partnership? What would make them work together selflessly, even when their own congregations might not benefit at all?

To answer those questions, we need to dig deeper into the Jerusalem collection partnership. We need to look at what drove Paul and the Gentile churches to join together for the benefit of a faraway group of foreign people many of them had never met. On the face of things, the Jerusalem collection just made no sense.

Why was Paul, the apostle to the Gentiles, so zealous about blessing the Jews in Jerusalem? Why did he spend so much time and energy ministering to a group that clearly mistrusted him, probably hated him, and might even have killed him in appreciation for the gift he collected for them?[1] Why did he set aside his burning desire to bring the gospel to Spain, the last unevangelized region of the Mediterranean, in order to take a two thousand-mile detour to visit Jerusalem and deliver the gift himself? Why did he risk his already-fragile relationships with Gentile churches in places such as Corinth and Galatia by pushing them to unite in a partnership that would bless the same people who often shunned them as less than Christian?

Let's start from the beginning.

---

[1] When Paul wrote about the collection to the Romans, he asked them to pray "that I may be delivered from the unbelievers in Judea, and that my service for Jerusalem may be acceptable to the saints" (Rom. 15:31).

The Story of the Jerusalem Collection

At the birth of the church (Acts 2), the first believers were Jewish pilgrims from across the Roman empire who had come to Jerusalem for the Feast of Pentecost. Many of them were staying with relatives in Judea, but after they were converted and started following the teachings of the incendiary cult leader (as many saw him) named Jesus, their families disowned them and put them out on the streets. In order to survive, these new believers were forced to depend on the generosity of people they barely knew.

Their new brothers and sisters in Christ responded! As they grasped God's generosity toward them, the early believers showed incredible generosity toward one another. Acts 4:34–35 says "there was not a needy person among them, for as many as were owners of lands or houses sold them and brought the proceeds of what was sold and laid it at the apostles' feet, and it was distributed to each as any had need."

But this happy community did not last for long. Only a few years later, a great persecution broke out, which scattered most of the believers in Judea back across the Roman empire. A small group was left in Jerusalem, but they had almost nothing. As despised Christians, it was impossible for them to get jobs and support their families. Added to this struggle was a great famine that occurred in AD 46. Luke described it:

> Now in these days prophets came down from Jerusalem to Antioch. And one of them named Agabus stood up and foretold by the Spirit that there would be a great famine over all the world (this took place in the days of Claudius). So the disciples determined, every one according to his ability, to send relief to the brothers living in Judea. And they did so, sending it to the elders by the hand of Barnabas and Saul. (Acts 11:27–30)

This was most likely the same mission Paul described in Galatians 2:2, when he said he and Barnabas "went up because of a revelation."[2] During this trip, they forged a strategic partnership with the apostles in Jerusalem:

> When James and Cephas and John, who seemed to be pillars, perceived the grace that was given to me, they gave the right hand of fellowship to Barnabas and me, that we should go to the Gentiles and they to the circumcised. Only, they asked us to remember the poor, the very thing I was eager to do. (Gal. 2:9–10)

This is the point where Paul's mission crystallized. While the Jerusalem apostles focused on reaching Jews, Paul and Barnabas would go across the Roman empire, planting churches among the Gentiles. And a major goal of their mission would be to "remember the poor" of Jerusalem by connecting the new churches together to support the struggling saints back there.[3]

After Paul and Barnabas returned to Antioch, they were commissioned by the Holy Spirit for this new mission and then sent out by the church. Over the next decade, Paul planted churches in four major regions: Galatia (Antioch of Pisidia, Iconium, Lystra, and Derbe; Acts 13–14), Macedonia (Philippi, Berea, and Thessalonica; Acts 16–17), Achaia (Corinth; Acts 18), and Asia (Ephesus; Acts 19).

Once Paul had evangelized a city, established a Christian community, strengthened the saints in the church, and raised up leaders to guide the church, he called the church toward part-

---

[2] While some scholars argue that Galatians 2 is actually Paul's description of the Jerusalem Council of Acts 15, it is more likely that Paul was referring to his "famine relief visit," recounted in Acts 11:30. Otherwise, Paul's chronology in Galatians (which refers to only two post-conversion visits to Jerusalem) and Luke's chronology in Acts (in which the Jerusalem Council is Paul's third post-conversion visit) disagree. Apart from the chronological issues, the dispute between Paul and Peter, described in Galatians 2, seems more likely to have been one of the causes of the Jerusalem Council rather than the result of it.

[3] The "poor" Paul was referring to here were almost certainly the poor saints in Jerusalem. In Romans 15:26, Paul referred to "the poor among the saints at Jerusalem." See F. F. Bruce, *The Epistle to the Galatians*, New International Greek Testament Commentary (Grand Rapids: Eerdmans, 1982), 126.

nership in God's greater kingdom.[4] And there was one major task he recruited each of the churches he planted to carry out: collecting money for the poor in Jerusalem.

After spending ten years planting churches, strengthening churches, connecting churches, and collecting from churches, Paul decided it was finally time to deliver the big gift. This obviously wasn't an impulsive effort. He traveled one thousand miles to take the collection to the church in Jerusalem (Acts 21:17–20; 24:17), bringing with him representatives from at least three of the four regions where he had planted churches.[5] The saints in Jerusalem received the gift with great joy and gratitude, but as Paul expected, he was arrested by unbelieving Jews soon after the gift was delivered. Paul was soon on trial for his very life.

The Purpose for Partnership

So what sent Paul on this kind of suicide mission? One thing's for sure—it wasn't to impress the apostles in Jerusalem: "Those who seemed to be influential (what they were makes no difference to me; God shows no partiality)—those, I say, who seemed influential added nothing to me" (Gal. 2:6). Neither was the collection some kind of tax imposed by the Jerusalem mother church on Paul and the churches he had established: "Each one must give as he has decided in his heart, not reluctantly or under

---

[4] As David Downs observes, "Embedded in Paul's epistles are numerous passages that highlight regional connections within Pauline Christianity, including greetings from members of one community to members of another (Rom 16:3–16, 21–23; 1 Cor 16:19–20; Phil 4:21–22; Phlm 23; cf. Col 4:10–17), letters of recommendation (Rom 16:1; 1 Cor 16:10–12; cf Col 4:7–10), references to travel delegates (1 Cor 1:11, 2 Cor 7:2–16; 8:16–24; 9:3–5; Phil 2:25–30; 1 Thess 3:6), and requests for hospitality (Rom 15:24; Phlm 22; cf. Col 4:19)" (*The Offering of the Gentiles: Paul's Collection for Jerusalem in Its Chronological, Cultural, and Cultic Contexts* [WUNT 2/248; Tübingen: Mohr Siebeck, 2008], 18).

[5] Acts 20:4 lists them. From the region of Macedonia: Sopater son of Pyrrhus from Berea and Aristarchus and Secundus from Thessalonica; from the region of Galatia: Gaius from Derbe and Timothy from Lystra; from the region of Asia: Tychicus and Trophimus.

compulsion" (2 Cor. 9:7). So what drove him to strive and strain toward a partnership of wildly different churches? What motivated him to risk his life delivering their gift?

There are at least three key motivations that propelled the first kingdom partnership, and these still inspire most partnerships today:

Fellowship and Unity. When Paul described the Jerusalem collection, he used many words. *Service. Gift. Privilege.* But one of the most powerful is the Greek word *koinonia* (Rom. 15:26). Literally meaning "sharing," this word is often translated as "fellowship." Paul saw the collection as a unique way to draw churches together and display the unity of the Spirit.

This wasn't natural, especially in the racially charged church of the first century. Paul continually challenged churches to pursue gospel unity among all Christians, both Jew and Gentile (Galatians 3; Ephesians 2), but the Jerusalem collection partnership was a powerfully tangible demonstration of how the gospel transcends race, culture, and tradition.[6] Paul made this purpose clear: "For if the Gentiles have come to share in [the Jews'] spiritual blessings, they ought also to be of service to them in material blessings" (Rom. 15:27).

---

[6] The Old Testament prophecies of a "pilgrimage of the nations" and the eschatological unity that it would produce were crucial in shaping Paul's vision of how and why the Gentile Christians should bring a material offering to Jerusalem. This common Old Testament theme refers to the future ingathering of the nations to God's covenant people. Of course, the expectation of blessing for the nations can be traced all the way back to the Abrahamic promises, such as "in you all the families of the earth shall be blessed" (Gen. 12:3) and "I have made you the father of a multitude of nations" (17:5). Paul was well aware of these promises and referred to them often (see Gal. 3:7; Rom. 4:17). However, the later promises of the Gentile ingathering in the Prophetic Books added another important layer to Paul's expectations. In Isaiah 66, the prophet speaks of the time when the Lord will "gather all nations and tongues" (v. 18). When that day comes, the nations will bring "an offering to the LORD . . . to my holy mountain Jerusalem" (v. 20). While scholars have spilled a lot of ink discussing the precise role of prophecies such as this in the collection and in Paul's eschatology in general, it is hard to deny that Paul had the eschatological pilgrimage theme in mind in Romans 15 as he described his travel plans and referred to the "offering of the Gentiles" (v. 16).

And not only did the collection unite Gentiles and Jews, but it also bonded Gentile churches *to one another*. When Paul wrote to the Corinthian church about the collection, he told the story of the churches in Macedonia: "For in a severe test of affliction, their abundance of joy and their extreme poverty have overflowed in a wealth of generosity on their part. For they gave according to their means, as I can testify, and beyond their means, of their own accord" (2 Cor. 8:2–3). This "reminded the members of these congregations that they were partners in the gospel with one another, no less than with the poor among the saints in Jerusalem."[7] When churches work side by side with one another, they are reminded of their union with one another in Christ.

Evangelism. When Paul delivered the Jerusalem collection, there's a strong possibility that he was blessing not only needy Christians but also needy unbelievers. After he was arrested in Jerusalem, he testified before the Roman governor, Felix, and said: "I came to bring alms *to my nation* and to present offerings. While I was doing this, they found me purified in the temple, without any crowd or tumult" (Acts 24:17–18). Paul may have given most of the collection to the church in Jerusalem, but he probably gave a portion of it to the temple for distribution to needy unbelieving Jews. Why did he do this? One reason: "Brothers, my heart's desire and prayer to God for [the Jews] is that they may be saved" (Rom. 10:1).[8]

Paul knew he couldn't accomplish this goal by himself, so he established the Jerusalem collection partnership to get some help. Evangelism is hard enough even when you're simply displaying and proclaiming the gospel to the family members, friends, neighbors, and coworkers God has already put in your life. When you're trying to take the gospel to highly resistant groups and

---

[7] Downs, *The Offering of the Gentiles*, 19.
[8] David Garland makes a similar argument in *2 Corinthians*, New American Commentary, vol. 29 (Nashville: Broadman & Holman, 1999), 389–90.

highly dangerous places, it's just too much for one person, or even one church, to handle.

That's why a group of churches in Hawaii partnered together when they sensed God leading them to reach victims of the sex-trafficking industry in Waikiki. Most tourists don't stay up late enough to see the evil that emerges after dark, but every Friday night, believers from different local churches gather in Waikiki to pray for two or three hours. Then they walk the streets of Waikiki from 10 p.m. to 3 a.m., looking for prostitutes to engage in conversation. They offer to pray with the young women, many of them runaway girls as young as fourteen or fifteen who are enslaved by coercive pimps. These brave saints offer any assistance they can provide. Sometimes they have a chance to share the gospel, but they usually only have a few minutes to talk before a pimp swoops in to drive them away.

Over the last few years, this partnership has rescued almost a dozen women from slavery in the sex industry. The churches work together to provide safe housing and basic necessities for the young women and their children, connect them with loving Christian sisters and brothers who often become surrogate families, and disciple them toward maturity in Christ.

Compassion. When Paul wrote to the Galatians, possibly with the goal of recruiting them into the partnership, he said, "As we have opportunity, let us do good to everyone, and especially to those who are of the household of faith" (Gal. 6:10). Compassion toward the poor and suffering is natural for people who have experienced *God's* compassion. As Paul said to the Corinthians, "[God] comforts us in all our affliction, so that we may be able to comfort those who are in any affliction, with the comfort with which we ourselves are comforted by God" (2 Cor. 1:4).

In 2010, this kind of compassion drove two churches to establish a partnership to bring aid to Haiti following the horrific earthquake that killed hundreds of thousands of people and left more than a million homeless. James MacDonald from Harvest

Bible Chapel in Chicago and Mark Driscoll from Mars Hill Church in Seattle wanted to respond, but they quickly realized that not even their two megachurches could do much to meet the incredible needs in Haiti by themselves.

So MacDonald and Driscoll spent the next few days putting together a church partnership for disaster relief called Churches Helping Churches. Donations began pouring in from around the world, and less than a week later the churches had a team on the ground in Haiti assessing the damage, praying with the people, and helping Haitian churches begin the long process of recovery. Churches Helping Churches has given millions of dollars and countless resources to churches in Haiti and, after the March 2011 earthquake and tsunami, Japan.

In thousands of cities across the globe, churches large and small haven't considered the amazing things God could do through them in partnership with others. He used kingdom churches to turn the first-century world upside down (Acts 17:6). What will he do in the twenty-first?

Questions for Discussion:

1. What are some ways you've already seen God expand his kingdom through you and your church? How could partnerships enhance what God is already doing?
2. What aversions do you have to partnering with other churches? Do you have a fear of overcommitting limited time, resources, or people; a desire to maintain theological purity; or feelings of jealousy or competition toward other churches?
3. What motivations are driving you toward cooperative ministry with other churches? Fellowship and unity? Evangelism? Compassion? Something else?

2

Laying the Foundation

Building on the Gospel

> *I went up because of a revelation and set before them . . . the gospel that I proclaim among the Gentiles, in order to make sure I was not running or had not run in vain.*
>
> GALATIANS 2:2

When you visit a church in America, you can usually tell within a few minutes what really drives the congregation.

The activity-driven church has a list of all its upcoming events in the bulletin, and you need a microscope to read it, because there are ten to twenty activities every day of the week. The experience-driven church sings every song eight or ten times, and when you talk to people during greeting time, they start every other sentence with "God told me . . ." The social/political-action-driven church has a table in the lobby with, depending on its political persuasion, either (1) family-values voter information guides or (2) fair-trade coffee that was hand-roasted by widows in a remote village in South America. The counseling-driven church has a rack on the wall advertising recovery groups for caffeine addiction and every other dependency under the sun. The family-driven church has entire rows taken up by families with five or six kids since there are no children's programs that might split families apart. The Bible-driven church hands you a bulletin as thick as your thumb, containing the pastor's seven-page sermon outline (plus fourteen pages of footnotes).

How many of those characteristics mark your own church? We can see three or four in our own! Few of these things are necessarily wrong, and many of them are attractive to us because they emphasize an implication of the gospel. God calls us to study his Word, to experience him through worship and prayer, to shepherd our families, and to influence our culture. The problem comes when you reduce the gospel to any of these things. Then your church becomes the family worship church down the street from the social justice church, rather than simply being a gospel church.

This kind of reductionism is a particularly strong temptation for churches that work together in kingdom ministry, because kingdom partnerships are usually focused on one specific gospel implication: assisting the poor locally or overseas; influencing one area of culture, such as the arts; or teaching biblical interpretation to rising church leaders. Gospel implications may be the focus of a partnership, but they cannot be the foundation. When a single implication of the gospel is all that's holding us together, rather than the gospel itself, the ministry will fall apart as soon as the money runs out or differences arise, as they always do.

Kingdom partnerships must be built on the gospel alone. This means that there should be a direct line between the aims of the partnership and Jesus's life, death, and resurrection. As the implications of what Jesus has done are worked out in our churches, we will be compelled to partner with other churches to make the gospel and its implications clear across our cities and around the world.

The Gospel and the Jerusalem Collection

When Paul traveled to Jerusalem to deliver the Antioch church's gift to the suffering saints, the gospel was his first concern: "I went up because of a revelation and set before them . . . the gospel that I proclaim among the Gentiles, in order to make sure I was not running or had not run in vain" (Gal. 2:2).[1] Every Christian leader talks about the gospel, but Paul wanted to make sure they were all talking about the same thing.

The gospel is the good news of God's victory over sin through the perfect life, substitutionary death, and resurrected reign of Jesus Christ. The gospel was proclaimed to the Serpent in the garden: "I will put enmity between you and the woman, and between your offspring and her offspring; he shall bruise your head, and you shall bruise his heel" (Gen. 3:15). It was fore-shadowed by the sacrifices of Moses: "He shall lay his hand on the head of the burnt offering, and it shall be accepted for him to make atonement for him" (Lev. 1:4). The gospel was experienced by Isaiah in the temple (after he had already delivered five chapters of Spirit-inspired sermons): "He touched my mouth and said: 'Behold, this has touched your lips; your guilt is taken away, and your sin atoned for'" (Isa. 6:7). It was preached by Paul above all else: "I delivered to you as of first importance what I also received: that Christ died for our sins in accordance with the Scriptures, that he was buried, that he was raised on the third day

---

[1] While many scholars argue that Galatians 2 describes Paul's later visit to Jerusalem recounted in Acts 15, this view contradicts his claim that this was his first visit to Jerusalem after his conversion. Paul claims to have come to Jerusalem on the basis of a "revelation" (ἀποκάλυψις), and this description fits the prophecy of Agabus in Acts 11:28 much better than the dispute that initiated the Jerusalem Council in Acts 15.

in accordance with the Scriptures" (1 Cor. 15:3–4). The gospel will be fulfilled by Jesus at the end of the age when he comes to reign: "Behold, I am making all things new" (Rev. 21:5).[2]

As Bryan Chapell summarizes the epic story of the gospel, "God has fulfilled his promise to send a Savior to rescue broken people, restore creation's glory, and rule over all with compassion and justice."[3] This means the gospel isn't just a visa stamp on your passport to show the immigration officer when you get to heaven. It should shape every facet of life and ministry *now*: "The gospel . . . has come to you, as indeed in the whole world it is *bearing fruit and increasing—as it also does among you*, since the day you heard it and understood the grace of God in truth" (Col. 1:5b–6).

Unfortunately, the gospel just isn't enough for many people. We're always trying to add something to God's grace. Soon, the issues that drive our churches (such as strengthening families, pursuing social justice, or even studying the Bible) can start to take on gospel-level importance in our minds. Don Carson reminds us, "If the gospel is merely assumed, while relatively peripheral issues ignite our passion, we will train a new generation to downplay the gospel and focus zeal on the periphery."[4] Before we know it, the periphery can lead us to create entirely new belief systems, such as the prosperity gospel, the full gospel, the social gospel, and many more "gospels" that seek to complete what some believe is lacking in Christianity.

In Paul's day, the Judaizing gospel sought to complete what some Jewish believers thought was lacking in the Gentiles' faith:

---

[2] If you have never spent much time considering the storyline of the Bible, pick up an overview such as Vaughn Roberts, *God's Big Picture: Tracing the Storyline of the Bible* (Downers Grove, IL: InterVarsity, 2004) or Chris's book *The Whole Story of the Bible in 16 Verses* (Wheaton: Crossway, forthcoming).

[3] Bryan Chapell, "What Is the Gospel?" in *The Gospel as Center: Renewing Our Faith and Reforming Our Ministry Practices*, ed. D. A. Carson and Timothy Keller (Wheaton: Crossway, 2012), 115–16.

[4] D. A. Carson, "The Gospel of Jesus Christ (1 Corinthians 15:1–19)," *Spurgeon Fellowship Journal* (Spring 2008): 1.

obedience to ritual requirements of the Law, such as circumcision. Paul was afraid that this false gospel had infected the Jerusalem church, but when he arrived, he was relieved to find out that the apostles proclaimed the same good news he did: salvation by grace through faith alone. This was confirmed when they did not require Titus, Paul's Greek teammate, to be circumcised (Gal. 2:3), showing that secondary issues and practices were not going to be the basis of their relationship.

This budding partnership would not be the club of the circumcised, it would be the fellowship of those redeemed by the gospel of God's grace. So Paul celebrated the new relationship this grace brought about: "When James and Cephas and John . . . perceived the grace that was given to me, they gave the right hand of fellowship to Barnabas and me" (Gal. 2:9).

The gospel unites leaders and churches in a way that no philosophy, tradition, task, or mission ever could. People who understand their need and their desperate dependence on God's grace are naturally drawn to one another, like beggars who huddle together in an alley where a five-star chef slips his best dishes out the back door every night. And that kind of gospel fellowship is where every great partnership starts.

Gospel Fellowship

Take Surge Network in Phoenix. It's a partnership of more than twenty churches that work together to train rising church leaders. They also host monthly pastors' seminars involving up to fifty churches and 150 leaders. But it all started with four pastors who simply decided to have lunch together once a month and talk about how the gospel influenced their lives and ministries.

The pastor who launched the partnership, Justin Anderson, says this step was crucial. Partnership projects can be a pain, he says. We don't need one more thing taking our time and our money. So you might not be completely stoked about an idea that one of your partners has, but if you're stoked about the guy who's proposing it, it's a lot easier to support the idea. Partnerships strain trust, Anderson says, so trust needs to be established in relationship before leaders can start to work together.[5]

Andy Krause, who has helped launch missions partnerships around the world, firmly agrees. He says it takes time to build mutual trust, especially in other cultures: "A memorandum of understanding means nothing if the relationship isn't there."[6]

I've seen firsthand how gospel fellowship can lead naturally to kingdom partnership. A few years ago, I was meeting regularly with a group of pastors in our denomination, the Evangelical Free Church. We enjoyed one another's company, but we weren't doing much together outside our regularly scheduled meetings. One day, the topic of missions came up. As we talked, we realized that all our churches were spreading money, energy, and prayer for overseas ministry haphazardly across the globe, with little strategic thought. Praying together, we sensed God calling us to focus our efforts and partner together in missions somewhere. As we compared notes, we realized that we were all engaged in ministry to one degree or another in Southeast Asia.

But there was a problem: We were working with all kinds of missionaries from all kinds of organizations with all kinds of ministry goals. How could we unite? There was only one way to find out: get boots on the ground. A few months later, four of us jumped on a plane and went on a whirlwind trip through Southeast Asia. Our goal was to meet as many of our ministry contacts as possible and look for ways our churches could partner in ministry there.

As we drank gallons of tea and coffee with dozens of missionaries and local church leaders in three countries, our fellowship expanded. We gained many new friends across the region, all with different goals, target groups, and strategies, but all united by the gospel.

---

[5] Notes from personal conversation.
[6] Notes from personal conversation.

Once we got back home, we continued building relationships over e-mails and video chats. Other leaders in the East and West heard about what we were doing and joined the conversation. Out of this gospel fellowship, a church-planting partnership was born, with the goal of multiplying healthy churches across Southeast Asia. We called it the Kairos Project to signify how God brought us all together at his appointed time. While philosophical differences, financial struggles, relational conflict, and outside persecution have all worked to split us apart, our gospel fellowship has held us together.

Redeemed for Partnership

God designed us and then redeemed us in Christ to relate together and work together. Pete Cavanagh, who is part of the Acts 29 church-planting partnership in Australia, sees the thread of partnership woven throughout the Bible.[7] In fact, he says the idea of partnership is fundamental to God's Trinitarian nature and our very identity as his creation. The Father, Son, and Holy Spirit have been in perfect partnership with one another for eternity. When God created Adam in "our" image, he also made him coruler of creation.[8] Then God gave Eve to Adam as a partner "fit for him" (Gen. 2:18). We were created for partnership, both with God and with others.

But Adam and Eve failed in their role as God's image bearers—his partners. Their job was to be God's representatives in the garden, acting on his behalf under his gracious rule. But they did not trust God as their partner, believing that he was not holding up his end of the deal. They decided to partner with Satan instead, hoping to gain what they thought God was depriving

---

[7] Our discussion in the following paragraphs is indebted to Cavanagh's presentation, "Partnership," at the September 2012 Acts 29 regional conference in Warragul, Australia.

[8] One of the best overviews of this concept can be found in Stephen Dempster, *Dominion and Dynasty*, New Studies in Biblical Theology (Downers Grove, IL: IVP Academic, 2003), 56–62.

them of. When confronted by God, they turned on each other. Their partnership with God was dead.

As you read through the rest of the Old Testament, you can see this pattern time and again. God entered into partnership with his people, making covenants with Noah, Abraham, the people of Israel, and David, and all these partners failed in their part of the relationship. But this did not end God's commitment to partnership. Since all the human partners in history failed to keep their end of the covenants, God intervened to keep the covenants for *both* parties.

When the Word became flesh, Jesus did what Adam, Noah, Abraham, Israel, and David could never do. He kept his side of the partnership perfectly. He went to the cross to bear the consequences of our failed relationships, and he was cast out of fellowship with the Father along with us. But he rose from the dead to reestablish the eternal partnership of the Trinity and, incredibly, to call *us* into their eternal fellowship as well.

In Jesus's famous prayer in the garden of Gethsemane, he asked "that they may all be one, just as you, Father, are in me, and I in you, that they also may be in us, so that the world may believe that you have sent me" (John 17:21). We are brought into fellowship with the Trinity and with one another *so that the world may believe* and join us too! As Cavanagh says, "We look for those who are also co-laborers in the gospel, so our partnership with each other for the gospel now draws others into partnership with us and God in a continual cycle until Christ returns."[9]

Active Relationships

The whole scope of redemptive history highlights one thing about God-ordained partnership: it's *active*! Adam's partnership with God included the work of categorizing the animals and manag-

---

[9] Pete Cavanagh, unpublished manuscript.

ing the garden. Eve partnered with Adam as "one who helps" with the mission God gave. Jesus took on human flesh, lived in poverty for thirty years, tirelessly ministered for three more, then joyfully endured the horrors of the cross in order to restore the partnership between God and man. The Holy Spirit now empowers us to be co-workers in the gospel with others who are partnered with God in the same way.

When God calls his people into partnership, it's not just to rub shoulders. Good relationships form the foundation and fuel for great partnerships, but too often fellowship is where it ends. It's important to understand that a network is not the same as a partnership:

- *A network is passive; a partnership is active.* At the end of a networking meeting, you'll come away with a doggie bag from lunch and a few new ideas to pitch to your church leadership team. At the end of a (good) partnership meeting, you'll leave with an action plan for, say, caring for foster families in your city.
- *A network is about sharing information, expertise, and inspiration; a partnership is about sharing responsibility.* Networks are usually loose associations of like-minded leaders, with a revolving door of people who come and go all the time. Partnerships work collaboratively, demanding commitment from leaders and churches, and holding them accountable to follow through with their responsibilities.
- *A network is focused on individual churches/leaders; a partnership is focused on the kingdom.* In a network, I help you accomplish your own goals, expecting you'll do the same for me. In a partnership, we work together to accomplish kingdom goals that we couldn't achieve by ourselves.

To be sure, we need both networking relationships and partnering relationships. Local networks don't usually provide all the expertise, information, and inspiration we need, which is why we lean on national denominations and wide-reaching associations. But it's tough to partner fully for kingdom work with churches that are thousands of miles away, which is why we need to be connected to like-minded churches in our own regions.

These active, gospel-created partnerships are marked by one driving passion: the kingdom of God.

The Gospel and the Kingdom

Some Christians don't talk much about the kingdom of God. They think it's a concept that's just too foggy and undefined. But as Graeme Goldsworthy reminds us, we can't talk meaningfully about the gospel without talking about our resurrected Lord and King. As a result, "the gospel of our salvation is, of necessity, the gospel of the kingdom."[10] We should be celebrating and proclaiming the kingship of Jesus wherever we can!

Some Christians don't think we can have any influence over the kingdom's expansion:

> The kingdom is what it is. It does not expand. It does not increase. It does not grow. But the kingdom can break in more and more. Think of it like the sun. When the clouds part on a cloudy day we don't say, "the sun has grown." We say, "the sun has broken through." Our view of the sun has changed or obstacles to the sun have been removed, but we have not changed the sun. The sun does not depend on us. We do not bring the sun or act upon it.[11]

[10] Graeme Goldsworthy, "The Kingdom of God as Hermeneutic Grid," *Southern Baptist Journal of Theology* 12 (2008): 7.

[11] Kevin DeYoung, "Does the Kingdom Grow?" blog post, Feb. 15, 2011, http://thegospelcoalition.org/blogs/kevindeyoung/2011/02/15/does-the-kingdom-grow/ (accessed Dec. 27, 2012). In personal correspondence, DeYoung added, "The presence of the kingdom can infiltrate more of our world, just like the rays of the sun can break through the clouds and shine upon us with greater intensity." He is still uncomfortable, however, with the idea of the kingdom "advancing."

But in Colossians 4, when Paul talked about Aristarchus, Mark, and Justus, he called them "fellow workers for the kingdom of God" (Col. 4:11). Notice that word *for*. Does the sun analogy hold up here? Could anyone ever work *for* the sun? What could you ever do for it? So why would Paul say he and his partners worked for the kingdom? Why would he waste his time doing things that would make no real difference?

In some places where Scripture speaks of God's kingdom, it is talking about God's sovereign rule and control over everything. Psalm 103:19 is a good example of this sense: "The LORD has established his throne in the heavens, and his kingdom rules over all." This is why some people view the kingdom as a static entity. If God already controls *everything*, what could you ever add to that?

But that's not what the Bible always means by the "kingdom of God"—especially in the New Testament. Within the overall reign of God, there is a more specific aspect of God's kingdom that directly results from the death, burial, and resurrection of Jesus. Greg Beale explains it well (you might need to chew this over a few times, since it's so theologically rich):

> Jesus's life, trials, death for sinners, and especially resurrection by the Spirit have launched the fulfillment of the eschatological already-not-yet new-creational reign, bestowed by grace through faith and resulting in worldwide commission to the faithful to advance this new-creational reign and resulting in judgment for the unbelieving, unto the triune God's glory.[12]

Jesus's death and resurrection have established his reign as King over his new creation, and his followers are called to join in his mission to advance his reign. According to Tom Schreiner, the entire storyline of Luke and Acts points us to this part we play in God's mission. Jesus brought the kingdom through the

---

[12] G. K. Beale, *A New Testament Biblical Theology* (Grand Rapids: Baker Academic, 2011), 23.

Spirit (as recounted in Luke), then he poured out the Spirit (as recounted in Acts) to spread the kingdom through us. "In other words," says Schreiner, "the kingdom now expands; it reaches the ends of the earth through the work of the Spirit."[13]

That's why Paul talked about working *for* the kingdom. He understood very well that Jesus has given us the keys to the kingdom (Matt. 16:19).

The Keys to the Kingdom

Everyone knows that keys are a symbol of authority. Remember when you first got your driver's license? Car keys were power! Or when you got the key to your first house? That key was proof that you were the king of your castle.

I once worked at a large church with almost a hundred rooms. The number of keys you had was a symbol of how much authority you had, except it worked in reverse. I was the lowest guy on the totem pole, which meant I had to carry around a whole carabiner full of keys, one for every individual office and room I was allowed to access. The guys at the top of the organizational chart had only one key, but that key let them into every door in the whole church. I had to walk around playing "Jingle Bells" on my belt loop all day long—ching! ching! ching!—but they had one key to rule them all.

That's the kind of power Jesus promised us. He's not here in the flesh anymore to open the door of the kingdom for people— he's given *us* the keys. That means we have a joyful obligation to keep ushering more people inside the door, which expands the kingdom's population and therefore God's reign.[14] And, if you can believe this, one day we'll have not only the keys to the

---

[13] Thomas R. Schreiner, *The King in His Beauty: A Biblical Theology of the Old and New Testaments* (Grand Rapids: Baker Academic, 2013), 509.

[14] That is why the elders in Revelation 5 can say, "You have made them a kingdom and priests to our God, and they shall reign on the earth" (v. 10). The kingdom expands as citizens are added to it.

kingdom, but a shared title to the kingdom along with Christ! "If we endure, we will also reign with him" (2 Tim. 2:12).

Of course, there will always be people who misunderstand the kingdom. Building on the kingdom teachings of Jesus in the Gospels and observing the many good humanitarian things Jesus did, they see the kingdom expanding anywhere anyone does anything good. They may have the best of intentions, but they fail to see that we cannot talk about advancing the kingdom of Jesus unless we understand the atoning death of Jesus. Don Carson explains:

> Many writers begin with the expression "the gospel of the kingdom" . . . and then expound the gospel entirely in terms of what they judge to be central to the kingdom. Commonly this is carried out by focusing on the social and communal values of the kingdom, and the word "kingdom" becomes an adjective: kingdom ethics, kingdom justice, kingdom community, kingdom gospel. . . . All that the canonical Gospels say must be read in the light of the plotline of these books: they move inevitably toward Jesus' cross and resurrection, which provides forgiveness and the remission of sins. That is why it is so hermeneutically backward to try to understand the teaching of Jesus in a manner cut off from what he accomplished; it is hermeneutically backward to divorce the sayings of Jesus in the Gospels from the plotline of the Gospels.[15]

Without the gospel, we can do a lot of things, but none of them will really advance the kingdom. So when we talk about kingdom churches, we're talking about churches that are passionately committed to spreading the reign of Jesus as King. And, by God's design, this is done only through our demonstration and proclamation of the gospel.

---

[15] D. A. Carson, "What Is the Gospel? Revisited," in *For the Fame of God's Name: Essays in Honor of John Piper*, ed. Sam Storms and Justin Taylor (Wheaton: Crossway, 2010), 160.

So if you're going to be rescuing victims of the sex-trafficking industry, you can't be content to get a few girls off the street, get them psychologically treated, and get them trained for a new career. A partnership to assist the homeless can't stop with a weekly dinner along with a distribution of clothes and toiletries. Those might be the first steps, but they don't necessarily advance the kingdom.

Jesus didn't die on the cross, rise from the dead, and ascend to the throne of the universe to make things *better*. He came to make all things *new*, which means we cannot rest until people are redeemed and radically transformed by his grace.

What Kingdom Partnerships Look Like

A partnership that's shaped by the gospel of the kingdom will necessarily look like the kingdom Jesus described. He said:

- *The kingdom should be proclaimed continually* (Luke 9:60). Whatever good things we do in the world, we must first and foremost display the kingship of Jesus and call people to live joyfully under his reign.
- *The kingdom is owned by the poor in spirit* (Matt. 5:3). Kingdom partnerships work best when leaders and churches are poor in pride, selfishness, insecurity, and a sense of entitlement. We're always tempted to look for ways a partnership might enhance the reputation of ourselves or our churches, but a phrase I heard somewhere reminds me to keep this in check: "No egos and no logos." We're not working to put our own stamp on everything, but the King's!
- *The kingdom starts out small and may be slow to grow* (Matt. 13:31–32). The kind of driven leaders who launch ambitious church partnerships are usually ambitiously impatient. But Jesus has been slowly expanding his kingdom for more than two thousand years. Whatever small

corner of the kingdom God might use us to influence will also probably take a few years (or decades!) to develop.

- *The kingdom is gained by forceful people* (Luke 16:16). We're talking about people who aren't afraid to go through serious trials with Jesus for the sake of the gospel. As we'll see in chapter 5, every kingdom partnership encounters opposition at some point, from within or without. It's time to man up.

- *The kingdom gives more responsibility to those who use what they've already been given* (Luke 19:17). We know of a church of about a hundred people that's had a million dollars stashed away in its bank account for more than a decade. This church has also been slowly dying for more than a decade. Coincidence? Maybe. But when we fail to use God's gifts to advance God's kingdom, why would he want to give us more influence? Churches and partnerships thrive when they steward their time, energy, people, and resources wisely for the sake of the kingdom.

When Paul left Antioch for Jerusalem, looking to build a partnership, these were likely the kinds of issues he was investigating as he compared his gospel to that of the other apostles. He knew that the gospel of the kingdom changes everything in life and ministry, and it's the only thing that makes true partnership possible.

Avoiding Gospel-less Partnership

If the gospel is not fiercely guarded as the cornerstone of our ministries, it will quickly be lost. Paul Hiebert saw this happen in the church where he was raised: "One generation . . . believed the gospel and held as well that there were certain social, economic, and political entailments. The next generation assumed the gospel, but identified with the entailments. The following generation denied the gospel: the entailments became everything."[16]

The Student Volunteer Movement of the early twentieth century descended into the same tragic spiral. Stirred up by Dwight Moody's evangelistic ministry in the late nineteenth century, a number of young Christians banded together to form a missions organization.[17] These wild-eyed zealots had a passion for the gospel, along with an audacious goal: "the evangelization of the world in this generation." In the movement's early years, thousands of young men and women signed its pledge: "We are willing and desirous, God permitting, to become foreign missionaries."

From 1886 to 1920, the Student Volunteer Movement steadily grew, and the group sent out close to eight thousand missionaries! During these years, the gospel was highly valued and boldly proclaimed. But by 1920, the group had radically shifted its focus to the implications and entailments of the gospel. At its annual conference, G. Sherwood Eddy told the gathered students, "I heard a voice saying, 'Whom shall I send, and who will go for us to build a new social order?'"[18] The vital connection between the gospel and the kingdom had been lost.

Things went downhill fast. In 1934, only thirty-eight missionaries were sent out. The group merged with a number of organizations—first the YMCA, then the United Student Christian Council, and eventually the National Student Christian Federation. In 1969, the group, then called the University

---

[16] Paul Hiebert, cited in D. A. Carson, *Basics for Believers: An Exposition of Philippians* (Grand Rapids: Baker Academic, 1996), 26–27.

[17] This story is told in Robert P. Wilder, *The Student Volunteer Movement: Its Origin and Early History* (New York: The Student Volunteer Movement, 1935), 58–60.

[18] G. Sherwood Eddy, "The Significance of Present Day Conditions to the Students of North America," in *North American Students and World Advance: Addresses Delivered at the Eighth International Convention of the Student Volunteer Movement for Foreign Missions, Des Moines, Iowa, December 31, 1919, to January 4, 1920* (New York: SVMFM, 1920), 50.

Christian Movement, voted to dissolve. As one committee member said, "We no longer had any reason to continue."[19]

If we're not driven by the gospel, *none* of our efforts will have any reason to continue. Our achievements will be nothing more than shacks built of wood, hay, and straw. We must build instead on the foundation of "Christ and him crucified" (1 Cor. 2:2).

Questions for Discussion:

1. What gospel implications are you most tempted to use as gospel replacements (e.g., Christian activity, mystical experience, social/political action, counseling/discipleship, family building, Bible study)?
2. What kind of gospel fellowship have you experienced? Have you seen it move from relational networking to active ministry?
3. Evaluate some ministries you've been involved in. Were you advancing the kingdom through the demonstration and proclamation of the gospel? In other words, were you part of Christ's mission to make all things new, or were you just making things better?

---

[19] As relayed to David M. Howard, cited in Joseph L. Cumming, "The Student Volunteer Movement for Foreign Missions: Its Seeds and Precedents, Its Origins and Early History, Its Growth and Decline" (BA thesis, Princeton University, 1982), 199.

3

Clarifying the Mission

Identifying Roles and Resources

They gave the right hand of fellowship to Barnabas and me, that we should go to the Gentiles and they to the circumcised. Only, they asked us to remember the poor, the very thing I was eager to do.

GALATIANS 2:9–10

As I sat down for a lunch of snails and rice in a Southeast Asian nation, my stomach was more unsettled by what I was hearing than by what I was eating. The strong young Christian leader sitting next to me (let's call him Joe) had met a strong young Christian woman. They wanted to get married. But the leaders of the church to which Joe's fiancée belonged wouldn't allow her to marry him unless Joe was rebaptized in their church. They wouldn't accept the baptism of *any* other church. "Wow," I scoffed, "it sounds like she belongs to a cult." He shook his head and said: "No, it's a normal evangelical church. That's the way *every* church is here. We don't trust anyone outside. We don't relate to anyone outside. We don't work with anyone outside." I stopped eating—and it wasn't because of the snails.

In this repressive country, where less than 1 percent of the population is evangelical Christian, churches have experienced decades of brutal persecution. Government agents are constantly trying to infiltrate the underground house churches, so most of these congregations have hunkered down by themselves, almost completely divided from one another and even hostile toward one another, just as the government wants it.

That's why it was so heartwarming, three years after my snail lunch, to look around a room full of local church planters meeting together to pray, train, and prepare to lead a movement of new churches across their nation. There were more than a dozen bright, energetic, passionate leaders from all kinds of backgrounds, each of them bringing something unique to the table. The independent leaders, working fearlessly in dangerous areas, encouraged us to stay strong in the face of persecution. The Presbyterians, with their advanced theological degrees, helped us establish a solidly biblical foundation for our plans. The Baptists painted us an ideal picture of healthy congregational life in the context of that culture. And the charismatics made sure we were depending on the Spirit for it all.

As we saw in the previous chapter, the gospel brings together communities of leaders and churches who are passionate about seeing the kingdom advance as Christ becomes King over more and more hearts. We're talking about changing the world!

But there's a problem. Changing the world is an awfully big task and we're painfully small people, so sometimes we're tempted just to stop trying. Are we just fooling ourselves by thinking we can achieve anything? Novelist and atheist Kurt Vonnegut thought that way, arguing that all our grandiose dreams simply come from reading or watching too many epic stories: "Because we grew up surrounded by big dramatic story arcs in books and movies, we think our lives are supposed to be filled with huge ups and downs! So people pretend there is drama where there is none."[1] He believed people should stop trying to artificially inject earth-shattering significance into everything they do.

What Vonnegut never realized, though, is that every big, dramatic story we've ever read or watched was ultimately inspired by the grand drama of God's redemptive mission. And God has graciously written parts for us in this epic narrative. Most of us are just bit players, but each of us has a part to play in the expansion of the kingdom as we display and proclaim the gospel. When we carry out our little roles *together*, big things happen.

So what do our parts look like?

Paul's Burning Desire

Paul, being *the apostle Paul*, had more parts to play in God's redemptive story than any of us ever will. Apart from his role as the apostle to the Gentiles (there were only a few million of them to reach!), Paul had another commission—an ambition that was even greater than his desire to reach Rome and Spain. His most heartfelt burden grew from his most heartfelt sorrow: that millions of his fellow Jews were rejecting their King and Messiah, Jesus. Paul longed for his uncles, aunties, and cousins to come to Christ, and he was heartbroken about their condition. He went so far as to say that if it were possible, he would be "accursed and cut off from Christ for the sake of my brothers" (Rom. 9:3) due to his "heart's desire and prayer to God . . . that they may be saved" (10:1). Also hoping to push Jewish Christians past ethnocentric faith (3:27–30), Paul's mission was to disciple *all Jews* with the gospel.

---

[1] As recounted by Derek Sivers from a lecture given by Vonnegut. Notes available at http://sivers.org/drama (accessed Jan. 28, 2013).

To accomplish this mission to the Jews, Paul established a surprising sequence of goals:

> Bring the spiritual riches of the gospel to Gentiles (Rom. 11:12)
>   ➡ in order to make the Jews jealous (11:11)
>   ➡ and to bless the Jews with material riches (15:27).

To achieve these goals, even the unstoppable Paul needed partners who would provide human, material, and spiritual resources. That's where the Jerusalem collection partnership began.

Climbing the Mountain

It might be helpful to think about a kingdom partnership as a mountain-climbing expedition.[2] There's a mountain somewhere that God is calling you to climb, but this expedition is way too big an undertaking for one church to handle alone. You need partners.

Once you have the peak in your sights and teammates by your side, you still need to decide which route you'll take to get to the top. There might be some paths that are well-worn from previous climbers and other sections where you'll need to blaze your own trail. These paths are the specific goals that must be accomplished through Christ's power in order to achieve the mission.

Before you leave, you need to gather provisions for the journey. What are they? People? Resources? Experience? Connections? Who will provide them?

Of course, a plan for something as ambitious as climbing a mountain has to be flexible. You'll encounter unexpected storms, perhaps come across a rockslide blocking a previously accessible path, or realize halfway up that you need warmer clothes

---

[2] We're indebted to Scott Thomas and Tom Wood for this great analogy. See their book *Gospel Coach: Shepherding Leaders to Glorify God* (Grand Rapids: Zondervan, 2012).

and more rope. An ambitious partnership plan will be similar. Major and minor adjustments will always be required along the way, because God is sovereign over your plan and you are not. So remember Proverbs 16:9 when planning: "The heart of man plans his way, but the LORD establishes his steps." Even when God changes your established plan, it is always easier than making it up as you go along.

Mission: A unique calling from God that's bigger than your church can handle alone.

"What mountain is God directing us to climb?"

Goals: Big things that must be accomplished through the power of Christ to achieve the mission.

"What paths should we take to reach the summit?"

Resources: The gifts, expertise, material resources, experience, and connections needed.

"What provisions do we need? Who will provide them?"

Identifying the Mission

Some kingdom partnerships quickly coalesce around a common mission that has already been established. Others slowly develop out of long-term gospel fellowship. Like-minded leaders and churches who enjoy *being* together realize that God is calling them to *do* something together. But what exactly?

As a new partnership establishes its mission (or an existing partnership reclarifies its mission), we've found there are three essential ingredients to consider: need, opportunity, and congruity.

Need. Are there people in physical or emotional need who could be served effectively by a group of churches? Is there a crisis you could respond to with long-term ministry? Are there underreached geographical areas, people groups, or segments of the culture where the gospel has not yet penetrated effectively? Are there places where more churches should be planted? Are there leaders who are not being equipped sufficiently?

The Jerusalem collection partnership was launched when Paul and the Antioch church heard about the plight of needy Jews in Jerusalem and wanted to help. Similarly, the Western churches of the Kairos Project partnership saw a desperate need for more healthy churches in Joe's Southeast Asian country and looked for ways to address that need. Could we train more planters? Help them reach their communities? Give them seed money to help them get their churches off the ground? Provide coaching along the way?

Opportunity. It's crucial to understand that not every need presents an immediate opportunity for ministry. Proverbs 25:20 warns, "Whoever sings songs to a heavy heart is like one who takes off a garment on a cold day, and like vinegar on soda." Try mixing vinegar and baking soda at home (put on some safety goggles first!) and you'll see how our attempts to bring help and hope can often lead to violently unexpected results. We need to make sure we can actually be a blessing. Are there people who are asking for practical help? Are there unbelievers who are ready to receive Christ? Are there churches or believers who are asking for training and expertise? Are there unusual opportunities that may not last for long?

When Paul brought the first gift to Jerusalem, the apostles there asked him directly to continue in his ministry to the poor (Gal. 2:10). He saw a clear invitation to help fellow believers and to use money as an inroad to reach unbelieving Jews who had "a zeal for God, but not according to knowledge" (Rom. 10:2). The Kairos partnership in Southeast Asia was similarly invited to help a new indigenous church-planting movement by providing training, coaching, and short-term teams to support the local planters. We jumped quickly on the invitation, seeing a unique opportunity in Joe's country: the strongly authoritarian government was starting to relax social and religious restrictions in order to attract financial investment from the West, but money had not yet become God in the culture.

Congruity. Kingdom partnerships require multiple churches that are equally committed. This is not the same as being equally *involved*, as we'll see later in this chapter. While we may all have different tasks, we need to be in the battle together. Are there other leaders and churches who share the same burden as you to meet the need you've identified? Are they willing to invest time, energy, and resources? Do they have a strong passion for this ministry, or could it be that you're dragging them into partnership by sheer force of personality and persuasion? Answering these questions up front will help avoid painful conversations later, when unmet expectations can be exponentially more disastrous.

Paul commented on how Peter, James, and John all shared an equal burden for the poor in Jerusalem: "They asked us to remember the poor, the very thing I was eager to do" (Gal. 2:10). And around the same time as Paul wrote to the Galatians, James was also writing about how compassion for the poor and neglected is a natural part of gospel life (James 1:27; 2:15–16).[3] He believed that caring for poor believers and unbelievers was an essential part of being a follower of Jesus, just as Paul preached: "As we have opportunity, let us do good to everyone, and especially to those who are of the household of faith" (Gal. 6:10).

As you look around at your potential partners, it could be that, like Paul and the other apostles, you are beginning to see some needs, opportunities, and even some common ministry goals. But before you rush out the doors and get to work, you need to make some Spirit-guided, prayer-soaked plans.

---

[3] If we assume an early date for Galatians, both that letter and James were likely written in the late 40s.

Establishing Goals

You might see a mountain peak clearly in the distance and you might have partners who are ready to charge the hill with you, but you still need to decide how to get to the top. What paths will you take? What milestones will you set to ensure you stay on course? These are the goals that must be accomplished by God's strength in order to achieve the mission.

Remember, we are not talking about making a savvy business plan. There are times when our goals fly in the face of conventional wisdom, since the wisdom of the cross is foolishness to those who are perishing (1 Cor. 1:18). But Proverbs 6 rebukes people who don't plan ahead. Goals are essential, even if they're as surprisingly roundabout as the ones Paul put in place to reach the Jews. Our goals just need to be in submission to the wisdom of God and held with a loose hand.

If you've taken any kind of leadership class, you've undoubtedly learned how to set SMART goals. This concept has some value, but we'd like to take the liberty of tweaking it to reflect the sovereignty of God and the finished work of Christ. We think the goals set by our ministries should be:

- *Specific, but not legalistic.* Ministry partners need to agree on what they want to achieve together and how they're going to do it. But they also need to remember that their plans might be subject to the Spirit's veto (Acts 16:6) or Satan's schemes (1 Thess. 2:18).
- *Measurable, but not results-driven.* Ministries should keep track of their progress so they can judge whether their strategies are effective or not. But they can't allow their identities and feelings of success to be wrapped up in the results of their ministry. Moses was called by God to a strategy that would initially fail but ultimately be used to bring greater glory to God: "Your brother Aaron shall tell Pharaoh to let the people of Israel go out of his

land. But . . . Pharaoh will not listen to you. Then I will lay my hand on Egypt and bring my hosts, my people the children of Israel, out of the land of Egypt by great acts of judgment" (Ex. 7:2–4).

- *Attainable, but not without God's power.* Sharing the gospel with every person in Africa isn't an attainable goal. Planting a gospel-driven church in every major city in Africa might be, but to do it, you need God's power. Ministries should have goals that can actually be accomplished, but still, if it can be done without God, let the Rotary Club do it.

- *Relevant, but not limiting.* An organizational consultant might say that relevant goals answer yes to questions such as: "Is this worthwhile? Is it the right time? Does this match our other goals? Are we the right people?" These are good questions to ask, but ministries aren't always able to answer yes to all of them. No one would have said the twelve disciples were the right men to lead a worldwide missionary movement, but God often chooses what is foolish and weak in the world to shame the wise and strong.

- *Timely, but not irresponsible.* Time-based goals can bring much-needed urgency to the task, but they can also lead us to overlook problems in leaders, churches, structures, and plans for the sake of achieving our goals on time. We cannot sacrifice the health of people, congregations, or ministries for expediency. The Jerusalem collection partnership took *ten long years* to deliver its gift to the needy in Jerusalem, because it took that much time for the Gentile churches to grow and mature to the place where they could joyfully send resources and people.

Finding the Right Resources

When teams set off to lead climbers up Mount Kilimanjaro in Africa, everyone is given a specific role to play. There are cooks, who make sure everyone is getting something to eat; porters, who look out for the equipment; assistant guides, who help lead the way up but may be lacking in experience; and the guides themselves, who have been up the mountain dozens of times. But everyone on the team has a crucial role to play. The same is true in a kingdom partnership.

Tim Keller says, "Christian leadership is mobilizing God's gifts to accomplish God's goals in God's way."[4] And Paul made it clear that God gives many kinds of gifts. If you've ever led or attended a church membership class, this passage is probably familiar:

> For the body does not consist of one member but of many. If the foot should say, "Because I am not a hand, I do not belong to the body," that would not make it any less a part of the body. And if the ear should say, "Because I am not an eye, I do not belong to the body," that would not make it any less a part of the body. If the whole body were an eye, where would be the sense of hearing? If the whole body were an ear, where would be the sense of smell? But as it is, God arranged the members in the body, each one of them, as he chose. If all were a single member, where would the body be? As it is, there are many parts, yet one body. (1 Cor. 12:14–20)

Paul was obviously talking about individual members of a local church. But could it be that the same principle applies to churches working together in a kingdom partnership? Some churches are larger and better off financially. They could play a leading role in funding the project. Another might have pastors with a particular knack for theology (and maybe a few more letters behind their names than everyone else). They could help the partnership think theologically about some of the challenges it will face.

---

[4] Tim Keller, "Ministry and Character," http://timothykeller.com/images/uploads/pdf/Ministry_and_Character.pdf (accessed Jan. 28, 2013).

Every healthy church must fulfill some basic functions and should individually reflect the wonderful diversity of the body of Christ.[5] We don't have the freedom to decide for ourselves what part of the body we want to be or not to be. Still, God in his sovereignty does seem to equip certain churches in unique ways, positioning them for particular ministry tasks.

In the Jerusalem collection partnership, Paul and the other apostles recognized that there were diverse gifts and strategies for fulfilling the mission. Paul and Barnabas would go to the Gentiles, while Peter, James, and John would go to the Jews (Gal. 2:9).[6] Paul would establish churches around the Roman empire, and those churches would then send money and people to bless the Jerusalem church. The Jerusalem apostles would then distribute the money so it would be used most effectively. Peter wasn't very good at dealing with Gentiles, and Paul wasn't very popular with Jews, but together they advanced God's kingdom among Jews *and* Gentiles.

Uniquely Gifted

There are many ways God equips churches to provide certain resources and fulfill certain ministry tasks.

Unique gifts, strengths, expertise, or availability. There are people in each church with particularly strong spiritual gifts, wisdom, and skills gained in ministry or secular jobs, along with uniquely suitable schedules. There may not be avenues in each local church for each of these unique strengths to be used (which means they may remain undiscovered), but a partnership

---

[5] If you are not sure what a healthy church looks like, we recommend you read Mark Dever, *Nine Marks of a Healthy Church* (Wheaton: Crossway, 2004), and Steve Timmis and Tim Chester, *Total Church: A Radical Reshaping around Gospel and Community* (Wheaton: Crossway, 2008).

[6] Like Paul, James labored for decades for the salvation of his fellow Jews. Richard Bauckham argues that James's ministry in Jerusalem likely had an influence among both Jews in Jerusalem and Jews in the Diaspora (*James*, New Testament Readings [London: Routledge, 1999], 18–21).

might be what finally frees some people to use the gifts God has given them. "Sitting in your church each Sunday are dozens, hundreds, maybe thousands of people with gifts and expertise that will never be used for Kingdom purposes until you unleash them," says partnership expert Ellen Livingood.[7]

Unique resources. Some churches (often older, established congregations) have more money than they know what to do with. Other churches have properties in strategic locations that aren't being used much or good-quality equipment that's sitting in a closet. When invested in a partnership, these resources can bear eternal fruit as they help ease suffering, help reach people with the gospel, and help strengthen leaders and churches.

Unique experience. There may be a leader in one church with specialized training or education that will allow him to oversee one aspect of the partnership. Another church might have past involvement in a ministry similar to what the partnership is pursuing.

Unique connections. In a partnership to reach professional musicians in a city, one church might have a number of professional musicians who attend. These artists can act as a bridge to the target group. Another church with lots of businessmen might have connections to wealthy, community-minded benefactors who could sponsor community concerts that would serve as an avenue for developing relationships with musicians.

Livingood observes: "Each ministry opportunity is different and may offer varying degrees of involvement. Linking churches can start with one or several levels and later add more. However, it is not advisable to begin at a level beyond your capacity and then retreat. This leaves partners in the lurch and destroys relationships."[8]

Of course, that's not to say that confusion, conflict, and disappointment can ever be fully avoided in any relationship. As the Heidelberg Catechism asserts, "Even our best works in this life

---

[7] Ellen Livingood, *Your Focus on the World* (Newtown, PA: Catalyst Services, 2010), 78.
[8] Ibid., 76.

are imperfect and stained with sin."[9] So when multiple sinners are doing good work together, it's inevitable that confrontation, repentance, and forgiveness will eventually be necessary.

Unity in Conflict

When Paul reminisced about the unity he established with the Jerusalem apostles (Gal. 2:9–10), he couldn't help but remember the conflict too: "When Cephas [Peter] came to Antioch, I opposed him to his face" (v. 11). Here's why: soon after Paul and Barnabas visited Jerusalem, they set off planting churches in Gentile regions,[10] believing that Jews and Gentiles were both called into God's covenant people as equal members in Christ. In that day, equality with a person was signified by eating together, so when Paul observed Peter and Barnabas eating separately from the Gentiles in Antioch (and, worse, influencing others to do the same), he was compelled to confront them because "their conduct was not in step with the truth of the gospel" (v. 14).

If we build our partnerships around the gospel, as we described in the previous chapter, then we won't be slowed down by minor disagreements over the name of a partnership, the speaker at our next conference, or the design of our T-shirts. But when we see others walking in a way that is out of step with the gospel, loving confrontation becomes necessary for the sake of that person, our relationship, our ministry, and God's glory.

The Kairos partnership is committed to confronting sin and disunity when we see it, but this can be difficult in face-saving cultures such as those of Hawaii and Asia. It requires radical love for one another that outweighs our love for a comfortable and copacetic existence. One time I made a financial promise

---

[9] Question #62.
[10] In Acts 11–12, Paul and Barnabas were near Jerusalem. When they returned to Antioch, they were commissioned for their first missionary journey (Acts 13:1–3). The confrontation with Peter probably took place after the first missionary journey and was likely part of the "no small dissension and debate" that led to the Jerusalem Council (Acts 15:2).

to a local planter before I had cleared it with the rest of the partners. I thought we would miss an important opportunity if I didn't act quickly, but I was bypassing our agreed-upon financial practices. Two of my partners lovingly confronted me, helping me see how my impatience had quenched the Spirit's work in building unity in our partnership, and possibly even damaged the self-sufficiency of the church I was trying to help.

Seven Conditions for Confrontation

After describing how he confronted Peter and Barnabas, Paul offered the Galatians an overall approach to confrontation and conflict:

> Brothers, if anyone is caught in any transgression, you who are spiritual should restore him in a spirit of gentleness. Keep watch on yourself, lest you too be tempted. Bear one another's burdens, and so fulfill the law of Christ. (Gal. 6:1–2)

In these two short verses, Paul gives us seven conditions for confronting a ministry partner about sin in his life:

1. It should be done between "brothers." This sets the tone for the conversation. You're family, which implies that you have an unbreakable bond with each other. No matter what happens in the conversation, your commitment to each other as brothers and sisters in Christ will remain.
2. The other person must be "caught in transgression." The sin must be clear and present, not just assumed and implied. This is particularly true when confronting someone's underlying motivations, which are extremely hard to discern.
3. It should be done by "spiritual" people. This means you need to be operating in the Spirit's power, not out of anger and frustration.
4. The goal should be to "restore" the other person to a healthy relationship with God and to restore unity to the

partnership. If your primary goal is to get the other person to stop aggravating you or to get him to conform to your personal preferences, you're not ready to do this. Go back to condition 2.

5. It should be done in a "spirit of gentleness." A harsh rebuke almost never brings someone closer to Jesus. It only erects walls between his people.

6. You must "keep watch on yourself" during the whole process. When the other person reacts defensively and questions your judgment, morality, and right to question him (as he might), you'll be tempted to respond in pride and arrogance. You'll want to start using all the ammunition you've been storing up in your mind over the years, reminding the other person about all the ways he's offended you, failed you, and disappointed you. Did you notice all those "you's"? They have nothing to do with restoring the other person, and therefore have no place in the conversation.

7. Be ready to "bear one another's burdens" over the long haul. The process of restoration probably won't happen overnight. Offer your ongoing love, support, and gentle accountability to your partner. Help him take concrete steps to overcome the sin through God's Spirit-empowered grace, which is the "law of Christ."

The further you get into kingdom partnership, the harder it will be to avoid differences and even conflict. But if, by the Spirit, you come out on the other side with your partnership intact, then you will probably start seeing God work in ways that you never thought possible. Remember the need and opportunity that brought you together, and work hard to see the gospel advance because of your shared commitment to the mission God called you to pursue. Anything worth doing is worth persevering for, as we'll see in chapter 5.

See the Need and Act on It!

Prayerful planning, discussion, and unity-building are crucial, but cannot replace Spirit-empowered action. Charles Spurgeon said:

> I believe in eggs, but we must get chickens out of them. . . .
> Brethren, do something; do something; do something. While
> committees waste their time over resolutions, do something.
> While Societies and Unions are making constitutions, let us win
> souls. Too often we discuss, and discuss, and discuss, and Satan
> laughs in his sleeve. It is time we had done planning and sought
> something to plan. I pray you: be men of action, all of you.[11]

William Carey, the father of the modern missionary movement, saw firsthand what can happen when a group of churches sees a need, seizes the opportunity, and takes action together in God's strength.

Carey labored alone in India for nearly twenty years to create a Sanskrit dictionary and numerous Bible translations. Then the unthinkable happened. In March 1812, the building that held Carey's printing press and books burned to the ground. Almost all of his translation work was lost. Nothing was saved in the fire. Many thousands of hours that had been devoted to the hard work of translating God's Word were wasted.[12]

"In one short evening the labours of years are consumed," Carey wrote the next day. "How unsearchable are the ways of God." But he could not begin to imagine what God was going to do.

One of the first to hear about the disaster was Andrew Fuller, the leader of the Baptist Missionary Society back in England. Fuller and the other partner churches of the society began to pray for missions like they had never, ever prayed before. Money

---

[11] Charles Haddon Spurgeon, "The Necessity of Ministerial Progress," in *Lectures to My Students* (Grand Rapids: Zondervan, 1979), 217.

[12] This story is related in Vishal and Ruth Mangalwadi, *The Legacy of William Carey: A Model for the Transformation of a Culture* (Wheaton: Crossway, 1999).

began to pour in. The news about the disaster spread beyond England, throughout Europe, and to America. Within fifty days, more than £10,000 had been raised, close to $750,000 today. Eventually, Fuller had to tell people to stop giving to the project. Not many partnerships have that problem! Just six months after the fire, most of the translation work Carey had done was re-created. Soon after, two new missionaries arrived in India. A year later, the British Parliament passed a law to encourage missionary work.

A centuries-spanning, globe-crossing movement of church planters, Bible translators, and Christian-aid workers was unleashed, all because a group of churches saw a need and opportunity, and did not hesitate to act on it prayerfully.

Brethren, do something; do something; do something!

Questions for Discussion:

1. What specific mission is God calling your church to pursue? Do you see a clear need and opportunity? Are there potential partners who share your burden?
2. What are the short-term goals that will help you achieve your mission? Are they specific, but not legalistic? Measurable, but not results-driven? Attainable, but not without God's power? Relevant, but not limiting? Timely, but not irresponsible?
3. What could each partner church contribute (unique gifts/strengths/expertise/availability, resources, experience, connections, etc.)?

4

Leading the Charge

Catalytic Leaders and Churches

We want you to know, brothers, about the grace of God that has been given among the churches of Macedonia, for in a severe test of affliction, their abundance of joy and their extreme poverty have overflowed in a wealth of generosity on their part.

2 Corinthians 8:1–2

Here in the Hawaiian Islands, we owe a big debt to kingdom partnerships.

In the late eighteenth century, Hawaii was devastated by civil war, and thousands of islanders were killed in the fighting. One young boy named Opukaha'ia watched in horror as his mother and father were slaughtered before his eyes. As he tried to escape with his baby brother on his back, his brother was killed by a spear. Opukaha'ia was sent to live with his uncle, a sorcerer.

At the age of thirteen, Opukaha'ia swam from shore and slipped aboard an American merchant ship. Convincing the captain to let him serve as a cabin boy, he learned English on his way to New England. It was there that he first heard the gospel and trusted Christ. Opukaha'ia was taken in by Timothy Dwight, president of Yale College and grandson of Jonathan Edwards. He soon began training for ministry with the goal of returning to Hawaii to preach the gospel. Taking the English name Henry, he began to rally his missions-minded classmates to return to the islands with him. But just as he began to gain partners, Henry contracted typhoid fever and died when he was only twenty-six years old.

His dream to see the gospel go to the islands did not die with him. Less than two years after Henry Opukaha'ia's death, Park Street Church in Boston commissioned and sent out the first group of missionaries to the islands. Partnering with Park Street, churches all over New England began sending more missionaries to join them. Over the next three decades, churches throughout New England sent twelve groups totaling more than 180 missionaries to the Hawaiian Islands.[1]

Within a few years, the islands were transformed. In what's now called Hawaii's Great Awakening of the 1830s, thousands upon thousands of people turned to Jesus in repentance. The church in Hilo quickly became the largest church in the world, eventually reaching thirteen thousand members. In fact, the population of Hilo grew ten times larger, from one thousand to ten thousand in a single decade, all because of the new believers who moved into town so they could be part of the church.[2]

---

[1] For the earliest account of Opukaha'ia's life and death, see E. W. Dwight, *Memoirs of Henry Obookiah: A Native of the Sandwich Islands, Who Died at Cornwall, Connecticut, February 17, 1818, Aged 26* (New York: American Tract Society, 1830). This book is available in many formats online.
[2] See Titus Coan, *Life in Hawaii: An Autobiographic Sketch of Mission Life and Labors* (New York: A. D. F. Randolph, 1882).

This transformation was sparked by the work of a kingdom partnership thousands of miles away in New England. And the fuse for that explosive partnership was lit by a catalytic leader named Opukaha'ia and a catalytic church called Park Street.

Catalytic Leaders

Kingdom partnerships don't ignite on their own. God typically uses a few key pastors or churches to provide the first few sparks. Pastors and churches who are already busy with thriving, successful ministries must pull together other busy pastors and churches to initiate, plan, and fund strategic partnerships. These catalytic leaders and churches are essential. While every mountain-climbing expedition has many roles, it's the guides who keep the party moving through challenges and around obstacles.

It is important to note that not every leader and church in a kingdom partnership should be the catalytic force. But from our experience and observations, there should be at least one of each in order for a partnership to thrive and multiply. This chapter will help you identify the kind of leaders and churches you should be praying for God to provide.

We've already seen that the clear catalyst for the Jerusalem collection partnership was Paul, who mentioned the collection in many of his major letters. He hoped to recruit all of the churches he influenced to take part. One of the most strategic churches in the partnership was at Ephesus, which likely served as a hub for the collection.[3] That's why it's in Ephesus where we can see,

---

[3] When Paul first challenged the Corinthians to join the partnership, he was writing from Ephesus (1 Cor. 16:8, 19; Acts 19:1–10). He gave the Corinthian church the same instruction on giving that he had already given to the churches around Galatia (1 Cor. 16:2) so he could collect the money and bring it to Jerusalem (1 Cor. 16:3–4). This seems to indicate that Ephesus was the hub of the collection (likely from AD 53 to 55). This is why Paul made a point to meet with the Ephesian elders, even though he was in a hurry to deliver the money collected from the partner churches to Jerusalem (Acts 20:16). In fact, the elders may have been meeting Paul to deliver more money collected from the churches in Asia. We

better than anywhere else in the New Testament, what kind of qualities and priorities made Paul such a galvanizing leader. On his first visit to Ephesus, Paul spent three years evangelizing Jews and Gentiles, establishing the new church, and raising up leaders (Acts 19). While there, he also started laying the groundwork for the partnership that would eventually include churches in Macedonia (such as Philippi), Achaia, Galatia, and Rome. He left Ephesus for a short time to receive money for the collection from Macedonia and Greece, then made a stop close to Ephesus on his way to Jerusalem to deliver the big gift. There he called a meeting with the elders of the church in Ephesus (Acts 20:17). Bringing along leaders from the churches of Macedonia, Galatia, and Asia (Acts 20:4), Paul was convening a sort of multinational leadership summit. Not just anyone could have pulled that off.

What are some characteristics of such catalytic leaders?

Catalytic Leaders Are Respected

It takes trust and respect built over the course of years in order to have the influence to convene other influential leaders. Someone who's new to ministry, or new to town, hasn't yet gained that kind of respect.

A year or so after planting a church in Honolulu, I decided it was time to start training other planters. Not content just to raise up guys from within my own church, I wanted to spark a movement of planters across the Hawaiian Islands. I planned a one-day seminar on church-planting and put the word out to dozens of churches. When the day came, five people showed up. Four of them were pastors I had begged to come speak.

I quickly realized that I hadn't yet established the respect and trust necessary to build the kind of partnership I envisioned. I was a young punk, and everyone knew it.

---

know from Timothy's presence as a pastor in Ephesus that the church remained closely linked to the "Pauline network" of church partnerships for many years.

That's not to say that you need to be old, grizzled, and gray-haired in order to build respect. A few years ago, I watched one youth pastor build a partnership of churches that would equip students to reach their campuses and serve their communities. As he did, he gained the respect not only of the youth leaders with whom he worked directly, but also of the senior pastors, who were excited to see the students in their churches doing kingdom work that wouldn't have been possible for their churches to do alone. Due to the leadership capital he built, this young man was asked to lead a new missions partnership that would involve churches around the world.

Catalytic Leaders Are Radically Dependent on God

Before Paul got to the leadership summit with the Ephesian elders, he did something strange. Luke wrote, "Going ahead to the ship, we set sail for Assos, intending to take Paul aboard there, for so he had arranged, intending himself to go by land" (Acts 20:13). The representatives from partner churches who were accompanying him to Jerusalem took a ship around a peninsula to Assos, but Paul decided to walk by himself for a distance of about thirty miles. Why did he do that? He clearly wanted to be by himself for a while, and the most likely explanation is that he wanted to spend some extended time with Jesus. He was doing a prayer walk!

Paul had many things to be anxious about: the crucial nature of this leadership summit, the constant possibility of conflict between leaders from different cultural backgrounds and theological persuasions, and the danger of rejection and even violence awaiting him in the hornet's nest of Jerusalem. So he took a day and took it all to Jesus.

Catalytic leaders always seem to have dozens of things on their plates that they could worry about. Our temptation is to come up with strategies to mitigate the risks and avoid the pitfalls on our own. But Paul knew that even when he faced a situation that seemed like a death sentence, it was God's way to "make us rely not on ourselves but on God who raises the dead" (2 Cor. 1:9). He modeled this radical dependency to everyone around him.

Catalytic Leaders Act as Role Models

When Paul sat down with the Ephesian leaders, he said: "You yourselves know how I lived among you the whole time from the first day that I set foot in Asia" (Acts 20:18). Throughout his meeting with them, he recalled actions he had taken and qualities he had exhibited during his first visit to Ephesus. He wasn't fishing for praise, he was reminding them of these things because he wanted them to imitate his model of Christlike ministry. Catalytic leaders must boldly and unashamedly embody the priorities and values they proclaim.

You can't lead people from behind. I've tried it. It doesn't work. A few years ago, I took my dad free diving through some underwater lava tubes from a long-extinct volcano on our island. After successfully leading him through a few short tunnels, I thought I'd let him take the lead. We took deep breaths, dove down twenty feet to the entrance of a cave a few hundred yards offshore, and squeezed into the tube.

Halfway through, there was a fork in the tunnel. My dad went the wrong way. I pulled on his fin to yank him back, but he shook me off and kept moving forward. I pulled some more, and he shook me off again. We fought back and forth for thirty seconds. Finally, my breath almost gone, I had to give up and let him go. I raced through the other tunnel and surged to the surface. I looked all around, but couldn't see any sign of him. Fearing the worst, I prepared to dive back down. Suddenly he exploded out of the water, gasping for breath. Somehow he had found a way out of the cave, but had had to squeeze through a tiny hole. Coughing and sputtering, he explained that he didn't know it was me pulling him back. He thought his fin was stuck.

The day I almost killed my dad, I learned an important lesson: leaders need to be in front. If you're leading a kingdom partnership, you can't just slap an inspiring vision statement and a list of core values on a Web site, then leave it to others to carry out the rest. You need to live out the priorities you proclaim loudly and proudly.

Catalytic Leaders Are Selflessly Humble

This might seem oxymoronic, but one of the most important priorities for a leader to display proudly is humility. As Paul reminded the Ephesians, "You yourselves know how I lived among you the whole time from the first day that I set foot in Asia, serving the Lord with all humility" (Acts 20:18–19). He said, "I do not account my life of any value nor as precious to myself," and he said his only goal as he ministered was to "finish my course and the ministry that I received from the Lord Jesus, to testify to the gospel of the grace of God" (v. 24).

Some who pursue kingdom ministry have goals that are a little different. They seek to build their own influence and power, or simply to make a name for themselves. While gaining respect is essential to building a partnership, it too quickly becomes the end rather than the means. Loathing behind-the-scenes work that doesn't build their reputation, some leaders are quick to volunteer for highly visible board positions and speaking gigs, but slow to do the long, hard work of patiently nurturing relationships and building leaders. They are made in the mold of Diotrephes, "who likes to put himself first" (3 John 9).

But what if we didn't count our lives or ambitions of any value or as precious to ourselves? Our ministries would look a lot more like Paul's selflessly hands-on approach: "these hands ministered to my necessities and to those who were with me" (Acts 20:34). What a great phrase: *these hands.* You could imagine him saying: "You, Stephanos . . . these hands helped you bring dinner to all the widows in your neighborhood. And you, Hezekiah . . . these hands helped you write your first sermon." Paul was radically generous with his time and energy because he understood that if you want kingdom influence, you just can't be selfish with anything—even your very life.[4]

Catalytic Leaders are Hard Workers

Members of the self-esteem generation in the West grew up playing games in which everyone won and listening to motivational speakers who told them they were all special. Many of them, now church leaders, believe that success in ministry is inevitable just because they're them. Then there are the winsome, charismatic leaders who think they can just charm their way to their ministry goals. They may leave a line of adoring grandmothers in their wake, but not much else. Besides them, there are the young, restless, (hyper-) Reformed leaders who believe they can just let go and let God in ministry. They want to kick back, drink a microbrew, and watch while the Sovereign Handyman does all the work.

But catalytic leaders understand that you don't just drift your way toward kingdom influence. As Don Carson reminds us, when we drift:

> We drift toward compromise and call it tolerance; we drift toward
> disobedience and call it freedom; we drift toward superstition
> and call it faith. We cherish the indiscipline of lost self-control
> and call it relaxation; we slouch toward prayerlessness and delude

---

[4] Paul was ready to face arrest and execution for the sake of the Jerusalem collection: "A prophet named Agabus came down from Judea. And coming to us, he took Paul's belt and bound his own feet and hands and said, 'Thus says the Holy Spirit, "This is how the Jews at Jerusalem will bind the man who owns this belt and deliver him into the hands of the Gentiles."' When we heard this, we and the people there urged him not to go up to Jerusalem. Then Paul answered, 'What are you doing, weeping and breaking my heart? For I am ready not only to be imprisoned but even to die in Jerusalem for the name of the Lord Jesus'" (Acts 21:10–13).

ourselves into thinking we have escaped legalism; we slide toward godlessness and convince ourselves we have been liberated.[5]

Like sanctification and growth in holiness, kingdom impact requires hard work.

The Western Text of the book of Acts says that when Paul first evangelized in Ephesus, he preached in the hall of Tyrannus from 11 a.m. to 4 p.m. every day. That lines up with the working schedule that most Ephesians followed in the first century. They would labor from 7 to 11 a.m., take a siesta during the heat of the day, then go back to work from 4 to 9 p.m.[6] This implies that Paul worked as a tentmaker in the morning and evening, and during his break time he preached to unbelieving Gentiles—every day. He probably worked fourteen hours straight, six days a week!

Paul himself confirmed this backbreaking pace, saying to the Ephesian elders, "Be alert, remembering that for three years I did not cease night or day to admonish everyone with tears. . . . In all things I have shown you that by working hard in this way we must help the weak" (Acts 20:31, 35).

Paul didn't say, "I did not cease night or day, except for Saturdays, because that's when I watch football, and Mondays, because that's my golf day." Comfort and leisure might be our highest priorities in the West, but catalytic leaders understand they need to repeatedly give up their precious "me time" for the sake of the kingdom. They work and pray unceasingly, as Isaiah urged: "You who put the Lord in remembrance, *take no rest, and give him no rest* until he establishes Jerusalem and makes it a praise in the earth" (Isa. 62:6–7).

Don't misunderstand us. We're not advocating overwork at the expense of family, friends, or health. Very few, if any of us, can maintain the pace that Paul kept in Ephesus. Every leader

---

[5] D. A. Carson, "January 23," in *For the Love of God*, vol. 2 (Wheaton: Crossway, 1999), 23.

[6] For historical details, see F. F. Bruce, *The Book of Acts*, rev. ed., New International Commentary on the New Testament (Grand Rapids: Eerdmans, 1998), 366.

must find his own stride to finish the race God has laid out for him. But there are a unique few leaders who are wired by God with a larger capacity to take on more and who may even have less of a need for sleep than other strong leaders around them. God often uses these kinds of people as catalytic leaders.

Paul worked hard, and in response, "God was doing extraordinary miracles by the hands of Paul, so that even handkerchiefs or aprons that had touched his skin were carried away to the sick, and their diseases left them and the evil spirits came out of them" (Acts 19:11–12).

We've all seen televangelists who want to send us a holy handkerchief they've touched, which supposedly will heal all our diseases (in appreciation for a seed-sowing gift of $50 or more). But there was nothing magical about Paul's handkerchiefs, aprons, socks, or underwear. These were the aprons he used to keep dust off his clothes as he made tents. These were the handkerchiefs he used to wipe sweat off his face as he stood at his booth in the sweltering marketplace.

The handkerchiefs and aprons were symbols of Paul's hard work, and the miraculous healings were symbols of God's blessing. God took Paul's humble sacrifice and used it for kingdom impact across the region. Through Paul's labor, amazingly, "all the residents of Asia heard the word of the Lord, both Jews and Greeks" (Acts 19:10). Dozens of churches were planted across Asia Minor during this time, some of which kept their doors open until the early twentieth century!

Catalytic Leaders Are Passionately Committed to People

Paul said he served the Lord "with all humility and with tears" (Acts 20:19). With *tears*. It's not like Paul was the kind of guy who cried whenever he saw a lost puppy in the street. He wasn't renting romantic comedies and sitting on the couch all night with a box of Kleenex in his lap. Paul was as tough a guy as you'll ever meet. He was whipped five times with thirty-nine lashes, was beaten with rods three times, was shipwrecked three times, and spent a night and a day floating by himself in the ocean, and it doesn't seem that any of that made him shed a single tear.

But when it came to the people to whom he was ministering, the spigot was open all the time. That's because he didn't see people as tools to grow his ministry; he saw ministry as a tool to grow people. He was passionately committed to them and their spiritual maturity, saying, "If we are afflicted, it is for *your* comfort and salvation" (2 Cor. 1:6).

As a result, the leaders in Ephesus loved him just as intensely as he loved them: "There was much weeping on the part of all; they embraced Paul and kissed him" (Acts 20:37). That's how people respond when you're passionately committed to them and self-lessly generous toward them. They're blown away, because there are so few leaders in the church or the world who live like that.

The Ephesians weren't the only ones who adored Paul. The Philippians loved him too, knowing there was no one else in the world who was so genuinely concerned for their welfare as Paul and Timothy (Phil. 2:20). While most Christian leaders were prone to "seek their own interests, not those of Jesus Christ" (v. 21), Paul and Timothy served the Philippians generously. The fruit of their labor was a church that became a model of radical kingdom generosity to the rest of the Christian world.

Catalytic Churches

Kingdom partnerships thrive when there are churches that are passionate champions of the cause. These are not necessarily the biggest and flashiest churches. While most of our modern Christian role models are megachurches and the celebrity pastors who lead them, it was not the big, wealthy churches such as Corinth that were the catalysts for the Jerusalem collection partnership. It was the small and poor churches in the region of Macedonia, such as the church in Philippi.

Whenever Paul wanted to persuade a church to join the partnership, he often talked about the Macedonians. He told the Romans about them (15:26–27) and bragged to the Corinthians about them:

> We want you to know, brothers, about the grace of God that has been given among the churches of Macedonia, for in a severe test of affliction, their abundance of joy and their extreme poverty have overflowed in a wealth of generosity on their part. For they gave according to their means, as I can testify, and beyond their means, of their own accord, begging us earnestly for the favor of taking part in the relief of the saints—and this, not as we expected, but they gave themselves first to the Lord and then by the will of God to us. (2 Cor. 8:1–5)

Macedonia was a region that had once been fabulously wealthy and powerful. The prestigious home of Alexander the Great, Macedonia had gold and silver mines that produced astonishing riches for centuries. But after 149 BC, when the Romans conquered and colonized the area, the people of Macedonia were essentially turned into indentured servants. Their riches gone, they watched all their hard-earned profits go straight to Rome.

By the time of Paul's writing, Macedonia was known for its extreme poverty (2 Cor. 8:2), even in a world where poverty was the norm. Most people in the Roman empire weren't completely sure where their next meal would come from, which is why Jesus taught his disciples to pray for their daily bread, not their monthly trip to Costco, where they could fill their minivans with weeks' worth of food. Everyone was poor, but Macedonia was *extremely* poor.

Compare that to Corinth. Many Corinthians were artisans and tradesmen who had regular sources of income. Paul told the church to set aside money once a week to send to Jerusalem (1 Cor. 16:2). This implies that most Corinthians weren't rich—they couldn't just write a big check all at once—but they definitely weren't poor. They did have regular weekly incomes they could tap.

The Corinthians had pledged to join the partnership for the relief of the Jerusalem church (2 Cor. 8:10–11), but these comfortable suburban saints were being out-given by the Christians living in shantytowns in Macedonia. It's often the case that the most needy people are also the most generous. The state with the highest per-capita rate of poverty in the United States, Mississippi, also consistently ranks among the states with the highest per-capita rate of charitable giving.[7]

Rich or poor, we have many different motivations that spur us toward generosity. For churchgoers, it might be a desire to repay the church for services rendered, a belief that God will reward us for our benevolence, or simply a sense of duty. Churches investing in kingdom partnerships can have similar motivations. They might selfishly give resources and people only to ministries that will benefit them, or they might joylessly support ministries out of begrudging duty. But the Macedonians had a radically different motivation driving their kingdom generosity: God's grace.

Catalytic Churches Are Empowered by God's Grace

Paul didn't point to any intrinsic goodness in the Macedonians. He didn't say to the Corinthians, "We want you to know how righteous and holy those saints in Macedonia are compared to you." He said, "We want you to know *about the grace of God* that has been given among the churches of Macedonia." The Macedonians were encouraged and strengthened by God's grace, and that allowed them to invest generously in the kingdom.

In Paul's earlier letter to the Corinthians, he said, "If I give away all I have, and if I deliver up my body to be burned, but have not love, I gain nothing" (1 Cor. 13:3). If your church embarks

---

[7] United States Census Bureau, "Persons Below Poverty Level, 2008," www.census. gov/compendia/statab/2012/ranks/rank34.html (accessed Sept. 7, 2012), and the Urban Institute, "Profiles of Individual Charitable Contributions by State, 2007," nccs.urban.org/statistics/images/CharGiv_07_1.pdf (accessed Sept. 7, 2012).

on any partnership out of any other motivation than the love
you've received from God, your generosity will quickly die. Ray
Stedman said well, "If God has not done anything good for you,
then for goodness sake, do not give him a dime."[8] But if God
has done something good, then it should show in every area of a
church's life, including the way we invest generously in kingdom
partnerships that may not benefit our own churches directly.

Catalytic Churches are Radically Joyful

Despite the persecution the Macedonians experienced, Paul said
that "their abundance of joy and their extreme poverty have
overflowed in a wealth of generosity on their part." Their kingdom generosity flowed out of their joy in the Lord.

It seems as if it should be the opposite, right? Usually we give
our time, energy, and resources away so we can feel good about
ourselves and have joy. I was once involved in a partnership with
a few churches for ministry to the homeless. Each church went
down to the park once a month to serve dinner, provide basic
medical care, and "talk story" with the men and women we met.
On the way home each month, we would pat ourselves on the
back. As in the classic *Seinfeld* episode, I thought: "I'm a really
good guy. No, I'm a *great* guy!"

But the Macedonians didn't need to artificially (and tempo-
rarily) inflate their joy level by sending their money away. They
already had overflowing joy simply from the grace of God in
their lives, and that motivated them to invest.

Catalytic Churches Start Small and Increase

According to Paul, the Macedonians started out by giving
"according to their means." In other words, they gave what they
could. If a family in the church made five denarii a week, and
they could provide for their needs with four denarii, then they

---

[8] Ray Stedman, "Guidelines on Giving," www.pbc.org/system/message_
files/4997/3690.html (accessed Aug. 29, 2012).

gave one denarius a week. They decided what they could live without and sent that amount to Jerusalem.

But then their joy grew to such a degree that they couldn't contain themselves. Paul said they gave "beyond their means, of their own accord." Remember, these were poor people with no credit, so it's not like they started maxing out their MasterCards with cash advances to send to Jerusalem. They proactively decided to drastically lower their own standard of living so they could give more. If a family was used to living on four denarii a week, they figured out how to live on three—then two—so they could give more to the kingdom.

Not everyone is graced by God with the ability to do this. Paul didn't even ask the Corinthians to give beyond their means. But some catalytic churches have been given so much grace that they decide, without any pressure from anyone else, that God is leading them to live more simply so that others can be blessed.

In Hawaii, a handful of small churches in the Gospel Coalition Network began to grow in concern over the lack of options for pastoral and theological training in the islands. Many local pastors could not afford to go to the mainland for seminary, and many of those who did never came back! So we partnered together to provide serious, church-based theological training for pastors and church planters in the islands. Investing increasing amounts of time and money into the partnership, churches and pastors gave up resources that could have been used for things that would have benefitted their own congregations more directly. Instead, they invested in the kingdom.

Within a few years, the Antioch School Hawaii partnership had been involved in training more than fifty students, most of whom are currently in pastoral ministry or heading in that direction. We prayerfully and unabashedly expect God to use these pastors and church planters to unleash another Great Awakening in a place that was once the most Christian nation on earth, but now sees less than 8 percent of its population regularly attending evangelical churches.

As you embark on a new partnership, be ready for the promptings the Holy Spirit might bring. Chances are, your church leadership will start noticing line items in your budget that seemed essential last year, but suddenly feel unnecessary as you consider the opportunities for kingdom investment you're now aware of. When you see extra income in your profit/loss statements, you'll stop dreaming about your next new hire and instead look for ways to send more resources outside your church walls.

That's what Twin Cities Church and New Life Church in Minneapolis experienced. A few years ago, they launched a partnership to minister to nearby prison inmates. They didn't want to start just another parachurch ministry; they wanted to establish a long-term, church-based discipleship program for both inmates in the prison and their families on the outside.

Seth Evans from Twin Cities was the catalytic leader who sparked the partnership. He had previously worked in too many prison ministries that made too little difference. Distressingly, he saw that 67 percent of inmates released every year were eventually reincarcerated. He wanted to bring the gospel to bear on this enormous cultural problem. Draining his 401(k) to fund a new ministry, he believed firmly that the local church was the only answer to the problem.

In his first year as chaplain, Seth saw eighty-three prisoners converted to Christ. Local and state officials gave him several awards for his excellence and effectiveness in working with inmates. Seth also saw the need for long-term, church-based discipleship and recovery programs in the prison system. In response to this need, the church launched Twin Cities Ministries, an umbrella organization for church-based prison ministry and other church partnerships.

The first congregation to jump on board the new partnership was New Life Church. They had already invested the funds necessary to free up Seth to serve as a pastor and the chaplain of the Ramsay County Jail. Now they wanted to get more involved. So three of their elders joined the Twin Cities Ministries board and the church committed more than $100,000 to support the work of truly rehabilitating former inmates through the gospel of Jesus Christ and the ministry of local churches.

There aren't many churches that could do this alone. But as the Spirit calls catalytic leaders like Seth and catalytic churches like Twin Cities and New Life into partnership, who can tell what the outcome will be?

You can build your own little sand castle or you can build the kingdom.

Questions for Discussion:

1. Catalytic leaders and churches tend to have entrepreneurial characteristics: they act as role models and are extremely hardworking. At the same time, they need to have shepherding characteristics: radical dependence, selfless humility, and passionate commitment to people. Which of these characteristics most describes you and your church? Which least describes you?

2. Paul wants us to know "about the grace of God that has been given among the churches of Macedonia, for in a severe test of affliction, their abundance of joy and their extreme poverty have overflowed in a wealth of generosity on their part" (2 Cor. 8:1–2). Have you experienced this kind of grace in your church? What are some specific examples? Practically speaking, how could this outpouring of God's grace overflow into those outside your church?

3. What would it look like for your church to start small, then increase its investment in the kingdom, as the Macedonians modeled?

5

Staying the Course

Patience and Perseverance

*This benefits you, who a year ago started
not only to do this work but also to desire to
do it. So now finish doing it as well, so that
your readiness in desiring it may be matched
by your completing it out of what you have.*

2 CORINTHIANS 8:10–11

In a province of more than six million people, you could count
the number of evangelical churches on two hands. None of those
churches was bigger than fifty people. Most pastors considered
it a great week when more than twenty-five showed up.

Quebec wasn't just resistant to the gospel, it was absolutely
hostile. Protestant Christianity was the religion of English-
speakers, who were resented by the French Catholic majority
in the province. If a French-speaking family in Quebec became

members of a Baptist church, they were no longer allowed to send their children to the Catholic-run public schools.

In this hostile territory, three men—Wilfred Wellington, William Frey, and Tom Carson—partnered together to plant evangelical churches. They went door to door, wrote letters, and gave out free New Testaments. But even the simple gift of a Bible was met with contentious rejection letters like this: "I am writing to tell you to no longer send anything to me because we pay little attention to your gospeling. . . . Your letters will not stop us from seeing our priests. You don't amount to anything in comparison with the church."

The new evangelical congregations remained painfully small, so more partners came to help. French-speaking missionaries who had been expelled from the Congo thought French Canada might be a good place to use their language skills. But none of them lasted longer than six months. They quickly questioned their calling to Quebec after seeing such little fruit compared to the overabundant harvest they had experienced in Africa.

Watching these partners leave, Carson's son asked him a pointed question: "Why don't you go to some part of the world where there would be much fruit instead of staying here and producing so little?" His father turned to him and said, "I stay because I believe God has many people in this place," and walked out of the room.[1]

There are sometimes good reasons to end ministry. Maybe you've reached your goal and it's time to move on, like Paul felt after he'd planted churches in every region from Judea to Italy (Rom. 15:19). Or it could be that you've prayerfully decided that a project is just too big and complicated to tackle, and you need some time to regroup. Maybe government regulations have made it impossible to work in a certain place and it's clear the Spirit is preventing you from speaking the Word, as he prevented

---

[1] This story is told in D. A. Carson, *Memoirs of an Ordinary Pastor: The Life and Reflections of Tom Carson* (Wheaton: Crossway, 2008), 41.

Paul from going to Bithynia (Acts 16:7). In cases such as these, it might be obvious that God wants us to turn back from our expedition. But, as Tom Carson passionately believed, we can't allow our progress to be halted by obstacles that God wants us to climb over by his strength, however long that might take.

As we make our way up the mountain together in partnership, we'll undoubtedly face challenges and obstacles along the path. These might include:

- *Slow progress.* We get discouraged when other partners don't commit as much as we hoped, strategies take longer to develop than we hoped, or tangible fruit doesn't come as quickly as we hoped.
- *Transience.* "Never count upon immutability in man," said Charles Spurgeon.[2] People move, have babies, get new jobs, and experience family crises. When these people are essential leaders in a partnership, ministry can quickly lose momentum, and even grind to a halt.
- *Other pressing priorities.* Things are always popping up in the daily life of the local church that seem more urgent than the "out of sight, out of mind" ministry efforts we're engaged in outside our churches.
- *Differences in ministry style.* Some people fly by the seat of their pants, believing that it's easier to ask for forgiveness than permission. Others want to meticulously plan every step and prepare for every contingency. Tensions between leaders with different ministry styles like these can make it awkward to work together.
- *Flakiness.* Most Christian leaders are, to one degree or another, people pleasers. We commit to doing things in order to make other people happy, only to regret it later. Then, still wanting to avoid conflict, we just let it drop

---

[2] Charles Haddon Spurgeon, "The Minister's Fainting Fits," in *Lectures to My Students* (Grand Rapids: Zondervan, 1979), 164.

rather than letting people know that we won't be able to fulfill our commitment.

- *Internal and external opposition.* Anything new is certain to face some pushback. Government agencies might make certain ministries difficult by requiring costly and time-consuming licensing. A few influential members of a partner church might question why their church is investing money in something that's not directly benefiting them.

Paul faced many of these obstacles, and many more, as he was establishing the Jerusalem collection partnership. To the surprise of no one who has read his epistles, the biggest boulders lay in Corinth.

Red Light, Green Light, Red Light

Paul first arrived in Corinth two or three years after the Jerusalem Council.[3] He did what he always did, spending every Sabbath in the local synagogue and preaching the gospel to both Jews and Greeks (Acts 18:4). After seeing many people saved, Paul continued to follow his typical pattern: establishing a Christian community, strengthening the saints in the church, raising up leaders to guide the church, then calling the church toward partnership in God's greater kingdom. The Corinthian church quickly joined the Jerusalem collection project, committing to give a significant gift.[4]

Paul left Corinth in AD 52, but by the time he wrote 1 Corinthians more than three years later, the church had still not fulfilled its commitment. The partnership stalled. To put

---

[3] The Jerusalem Council (Acts 15) probably took place in AD 48 or 49; Paul arrived in Corinth in the spring of 51. In the intervening years, Paul was busy evangelizing and, along the way, building the partnership.

[4] In 1 Corinthians 16:1–3, Paul discussed picking up the Corinthians' gift to Jerusalem. Since there is no hint about Paul convincing them to join the partnership, they had likely committed to this gift at a previous time, most likely during Paul's initial stay with them three and a half years earlier.

some pressure on, Paul made plans to stop in Corinth on his way to Jerusalem to pick up the church's contribution. When he had to delay his visit, the Corinthians delayed fulfilling their commitment. Even after Paul made a "painful visit" to Corinth, they still delayed.

So Paul wrote another letter to spur them on, saying: "In this matter I give my judgment: this benefits you, who a year ago started not only to do this work but also to desire to do it. So now finish doing it as well, so that your readiness in desiring it may be matched by your completing it out of what you have" (2 Cor. 8:10–11). This is the most direct command we ever hear Paul give the Corinthians in regard to the Jerusalem collection partnership: finish what you started!

Paul knew from personal experience that making promises is easy. Keeping them is much harder. There are always obstacles, challenges, and discouragements that keep us from finishing what we've started. The way we respond to these obstacles reveals the condition of our hearts, often uncovering diseases that lie deep within. These heart-level diseases weaken us, keeping us from making it up the mountain and persevering in ministry.

The Diseases That Weaken Us

Paul identified many of these diseases in his letter to the Corinthians, and he celebrated the way God had overcome these diseases in his own heart.

The Disease of Self-Dependence

One of the most common perseverance killers is the kind of disillusionment that sets in when unrealistic expectations are not met. You plan a big launch event for an exciting new ministry, but it tanks. You immediately start asking yourself questions like: "What did we do wrong? What do people think of us now? How can we get a better response?" After a few such experiences, it's easy for your identity to become more and more dependent on what *you* do rather than what God has already done.

That's why Paul reminded us that:

> God, who said, "Let light shine out of darkness," has shone in our hearts to give the light of the knowledge of the glory of God in the face of Jesus Christ. But we have this treasure *in jars of clay*, to show that the surpassing power belongs to God and not to us. (2 Cor. 4:6–7)

How well do clay pots hold up? Go to Israel and poke around any archaeological site. You'll find fragments of clay jars lying all over the ground. They're called potsherds: broken pieces of pottery that could have been made two or three thousand years ago. As old as these ancient relics are, most archaeologists won't even waste the energy to bend over and look at them, because there are just so many of them. They're everywhere! That's because clay jars and pots back then were like the Styrofoam containers we use today. They were cheap, fragile, and disposable. You would use them a few times, then just throw them away.

That's how Paul portrayed himself and the rest of us. It wasn't to denigrate anyone; it was to help us fully grasp the difference between the container and the contents inside. Compared to the treasure, we're insignificant, weak, and unattractive. We're Styrofoam! You can dress up a Styrofoam container with some nice artwork, but it's still just Styrofoam.

Paul was bursting our self-satisfied and self-reliant little bubbles. In 2 Corinthians 5, he used another metaphor: he said we're not buildings but tents. Three times he repeated it. How many hundred-year-old tents are still in use?

We're cheap containers carrying a 500-carat diamond. That's the size of the Star of Africa, which was cut from the largest diamond ever discovered. It was unearthed by miners in South Africa in 1905, and they wanted to send it to England as a gift for King Edward VII. They put a big crate on a boat, with dozens of armed guards surrounding it twenty-four hours a day, all the way to England. But the real diamond wasn't inside the crate. That was just a diversion. They put the Star of Africa in a cardboard box, wrapped it up with brown paper and a string, took it down to the post office, and sent it to London through the mail! The most valuable jewel in the world traveled across the globe in a flimsy cardboard box.[5]

Inside that kind of feeble container—us, our churches, and our partnerships—we have the same power that brought suns, moons, and planets into existence: "God, who said, 'Let light shine out of darkness' [in other words, "Let there be light!"], has shone in our hearts to give the light of the knowledge of the glory of God in the face of Jesus Christ" (2 Cor. 4:6). And the more dingy, dirty, and banged-up the box is, the better the treasure inside looks. It shows that the "surpassing power belongs to God and not to us" (v. 7).

The Disease of Man-Fearing

Any ministry eventually runs into opposition. You can count on it. Paul encountered opposition in Corinth toward him, his ministry, and the Jerusalem collection from the same people who often cause trouble in modern ministries: rich donors.

The city of Corinth was on a narrow stretch of land that connected northern and southern Greece. Sailors who wanted to avoid taking the dangerous route all the way around southern Greece would come to Corinth, pull their boats out of the water, and drag them four miles over land to the other side. Hundreds of ships were inching across the isthmus every day, which meant thousands of sailors were hanging out in Corinth every night, throwing their money away at inns, taverns, and other kinds of places your mother always told you to avoid.

---

[5] See the story in Joan Y. Dickinson, *The Book of Diamonds* (New York: Crown Publishers, 1965), 110.

The entrepreneurial innkeepers and tavern owners who were raking in all this cash became very wealthy, but they had a problem: they couldn't break into the old-money establishment in Corinth. Failing to get any respect from high society, they started looking for other places where their money could buy them influence and honor: clubs, charitable organizations, colleges, sports, and *religious organizations*. Some of these businessmen made large donations to the Corinthian church, and in return, they expected to have a big say in what happened.

This very small but very influential group evidently started asking Paul some very unfair questions: "If you're an apostle, Paul, why does it seem like you're always suffering? Shouldn't you have the favor of the Lord? And why are your sermons so boring, Paul? If you have the power of God, why are we always falling asleep? And you told us you were going to come visit us, but then you changed your mind. Is God really guiding you, or are you just making it all up as you go along?"

Paul wrote 1 and 2 Corinthians in response to these questions, saying he was "persecuted, but not forsaken; struck down, but not destroyed" by this group (2 Cor. 4:9). They could land some blows, but he always popped back up, kind of like the inflatable toy punching bags we used to have when we were kids. You could punch the living daylights out of them and they'd just bounce right back up. How did Paul do it? As he said to his accusers: "It is a very small thing that I should be judged by you or by any human court. In fact, I do not even judge myself. . . . It is the Lord who judges me" (1 Cor. 4:3–4). In other words: "It doesn't matter what *you* think of me, and it doesn't even matter what *I* think of me. We could both be wrong. What matters is what *the Lord* thinks of me, and that was settled at the cross."

This unshakable gospel confidence allowed Paul to endure harsh opposition, both within the church and without. Most of us will never be beaten with rods, stoned, or whipped thirty-nine times, as Paul was. But we might. Will we respond with

Paul's Christ-centered confidence and perseverance when we face opposition?

In Southeast Asia, we work with many brave saints who experience opposition and persecution on a daily basis. One house-church movement leader told us about a time when he received a letter from a church in a remote area that had been raided by the government. Police officers stormed into their service and beat the men, shoved the women against the walls, and threw the children out the front door. The letter from the church asked for prayer for the seven people who had been persecuted. This leader knew that there were more than two dozen people in the church, so he wrote back, asking why only seven were listed. The reply he received simply said, "We only count it as persecution if you're bleeding."

The Disease of Despair

When we partner with other churches, we do it because we've identified a need that's too big for one church to handle alone. It's probably going to be extremely complicated and confusing to figure out how to address that need effectively. Sometimes the confusion proves too much. We're tempted to despair and just to give up. Paul described it as being "perplexed" (2 Cor. 4:8).

The Greek verb translated as "perplexed" shows up only six times in the New Testament, and it usually means confusion mixed with fear or anxiety. When Herod heard John the Baptist preach, he was "greatly perplexed" (Mark 6:20). When the women went to anoint Jesus's body in the tomb, they were "perplexed" when they did not find him (Luke 24:4). And when Paul wrote to the Galatians, who were in danger of abandoning the gospel, he was "perplexed" (Gal. 4:20). In every case, the word points to a total inability to explain *what* is happening, along with quite a bit of anxiety about *why* it is happening.

We often get perplexed and anxious when we're expecting one thing, only to experience another. It's like picking up a glass that you think contains water and taking a drink, only to discover that it's soda. Or like the time Chris's dad put gravy all over his tapioca pudding. The food hits your mouth and your brain doesn't know how to respond.

During the early days of our theological training partnership, we got calls from many places across the state where there was a crying need for pastoral training. Rising young leaders were thirsty for instruction and mentoring. We met with many potential students who said they were ready and willing to jump into the program. Seasoned pastors in healthy churches appeared ready to partner as teachers and mentors.

But when it came time to launch, many potential partners suddenly went radio-silent. Others raised grave concerns over minor theological issues. We were perplexed. We had invested so much time and money in these places, and we thought God was working to expand our partnership to these new areas.

We were forced to learn what it means to be "perplexed, but not driven to despair." We had to come to trust God's sovereign hand even when our partnerships take turns that we do not expect or hit obstacles that we do not anticipate. Instead of despair, we learned patience and perseverance as we wait on God.

The Disease of Impatience

Any time multiple churches work together, there will be at least one church that wants to move faster and at least one church that tends to move a little slower. The faster-moving churches will start to lose patience with the slower-moving churches: "Can't you see the window of opportunity is going to close!?" And the slower-moving churches will lose patience with the faster-moving churches for being too reckless to slow down and do a little planning: "Can't you see the window of opportunity isn't really open yet!?"

In either case, we're in danger of losing our eternal perspective. That's why Paul said to the Corinthians: "Though our outer self is wasting away, our inner self is being renewed day by day. For this light momentary affliction is preparing for us an eternal weight of glory beyond all comparison" (2 Cor. 4:16–17).

When you read that, it might sound like we're condemned to endure a lifetime of suffering before we finally experience glory in heaven. It sounds kind of like *The Shawshank Redemption*, in which the wrongfully convicted prisoner Andy Dufresne had to suffer through decades of injustice in a brutal prison, then finally crawled through a 500-yard sewage pipe so he could escape and spend his last few years of life on a picture-perfect Mexican beach.

Earlier in his letter, Paul used the same Greek word to say he was weighed down beyond his strength with trials (2 Cor. 1:8). When this happens, it's easy to get impatient. If we're thinking only one month, year, or even decade ahead, we get impatient with circumstances or with other churches. But Paul said he was not only weighed down with trials, but also with "an eternal weight of glory beyond all comparison." (4:17). It's eternal. It's endless. It's mind-blowing! And it far outweighed the troubles he was experiencing. The New International Version translation points us toward this idea: "Our light and momentary troubles are achieving for us an eternal glory that far outweighs them all."

From a business perspective, time is money, and we're running out of both. In the kingdom, though, we've got all the time and money we need in the wisdom and riches of God. It took ten years of planting, strengthening, and networking before the Jerusalem collection partnership was ready to bring the help the churches had promised to the Jews in Jerusalem. Who has that kind of patience anymore? The average pastor in America stays at a church for only 3.6 years.[6] We don't have the perseverance

---

[6] Thom Rainer, "8 Traits of Effective Church Leaders," Nov. 21, 2011, http://thomrainer.com/2011/11/21/8_traits_of_effective_church_leaders_1/ (accessed Feb. 4, 2013).

to keep working with one group of people, much less multiple groups. We're far too similar to the Corinthians.

Common Stages of Partnership

Much of the impatience, confusion, despair, and anxiety we experience in any cooperative ministry can actually be traced to universal human traits and relational dynamics that spring from the way God designed us and the way our sin distorts us. In 1965, psychologist Bruce Tuckman observed four typical stages that most working groups experience.[7] We've seen numerous kingdom partnerships go through a similar process:

Forming. During this honeymoon stage, we're figuring out how we fit together. What goals will we pursue, and how long will it take to achieve them? How much responsibility, authority, and freedom will each partner have? How will we communicate with one another? Excitement is as high as it will ever be, because we're united around a common identity and common mission, but we haven't really gotten much done yet.

Storming. During this tumultuous stage, we're starting to accomplish a few good things, but we're also starting to see lots of problems. Partners aren't fulfilling their commitments. Responsibilities are getting dropped. Progress is slow. Goals are unmet. Philosophical and theological differences are causing tension. The mission is being questioned.

Norming. During this solidifying stage, we're creating structure. In order for a partnership to survive, systems must be put into place. Our decisions become more consensus-driven (and slow) than top-down (and quick). In order to maintain momentum, we defer to others and give up our own preferences and desires.

---

[7] Bruce Tuckman, "Developmental sequence in small groups," *Psychological Bulletin* 63 (1965): 384–99.

Performing. We're really sailing now. During this fruitful stage, our effectiveness increases now that our roles, systems, and best practices are solidified. As the ministry grows, leaders start to delegate more responsibility and authority. Conflict is to be expected and even encouraged as a means to sharpen one another and enhance the efficiency of the ministry.

Every partnership revisits earlier stages when things change. A turnover in leadership means readjusting responsibilities. A shifting ministry climate requires new systems. But gospel confidence in our status as treasure-bearers keeps us from flailing around aimlessly, as we're often tempted to do.

There's a striking illustration of this: the timeline comparing the logos of Pepsi and Coca-Cola over the years. Pepsi has attempted almost a dozen major rebrandings since 1898 in its fruitless efforts to overtake its competitor as the number one soft drink. Coke, secure in its status, has never changed its logo once since its very first bottle labels were produced. That's a powerful visual metaphor for confident perseverance.

Reasons to Persevere

Paul challenged the Corinthians to this kind of confident perseverance in partnership, based on the status and security Jesus gave them by lavishing his riches on them:

> For you know the grace of our Lord Jesus Christ, that though he was rich, yet for your sake he became poor, so that you by his poverty might become rich. And in this matter I give my judgment: this benefits you, who a year ago started not only to do this work but also to desire to do it. So now finish doing it as well, so that your readiness in desiring it may be matched by your completing it out of what you have. (2 Cor. 8:9–11)

In other words, our faithfulness and generosity in ministry are empowered by the faithfulness and generosity of God toward us. His extreme generosity was proven at the cross: "He who did not spare his own Son but gave him up for us all, how will he not also with him graciously give us all things?" (Rom. 8:32). Every one of us would give up *everything we own* before we handed over our sons, but God initiated his relationship with us by giving us his only Son *first*. Won't he also give us everything we need to serve him now? And won't he reward us when we meet him at the end of the age?

Paul reminded the Corinthians of this promise, and also warned them about the flip side:

> We must all appear before the judgment seat of Christ, so that each one may receive what is due for what he has done in the body, whether good or evil. Therefore, knowing the fear of the Lord, we persuade others. But what we are is known to God, and I hope it is known also to your conscience. (2 Cor. 5:10–11)

We will be held to account for everything good and bad we do. We can be spurred to persevere by this two-edged sword: we'll receive a reward from God for every word and deed that never got us any reward, recognition, or notice here on earth. But we'll also give an account for every idle word, unloving deed, and unfulfilled commitment. It will be burned up by the refining fire of Christ, even though we ourselves will be saved (1 Cor. 3:12–15).

Paul defined this certainty as "knowing the fear of the Lord." It means living in light of the reward and refinement that's coming. This doesn't mean feeling a need to prove ourselves to God. Paul said, "What we are is known to God," because God knows us and our inadequacy better than we know it ourselves, and he's already accepted us through Christ. But each moment, remembering that one day we're going to receive what we're due for what we do in that moment makes us simultaneously the most humble and the most courageous people in the world.

When we fear the Lord, we don't need to fear failure, discomfort, or what others will think about us. As the Puritans used to say, "Fear God and you have nothing else to fear." And when a group of Christians lives in light of the reward *and* chastisement of God, amazing things happen. That's what the early church experienced: "Walking in the fear of the Lord and in the comfort of the Holy Spirit, it *multiplied*" (Acts 9:31). The fear of the Lord isn't an immobilizing fear. It's a freeing fear, a joyful fear, a contagious fear.

That's also what Tom Carson and his partners in Quebec experienced. After decades of slow, humble, painful work, the gospel suddenly exploded across French Canada in the early 1970s. The number of evangelical churches went from forty to five hundred, almost overnight. The new believers who filled these churches were hungry to hear the Word and experience God together: Wednesday evening prayer meetings that started at 7:30 typically didn't end until 1 or 2 in the morning. Hundreds of young men were being launched into ministry, so the partner churches soon began to equip leaders and pastors together in a church-based theological training program. Within eight months, sixty students were enrolled. The harvest was plentiful and the workers were many!

Thirty years before, Carson had written a letter to potential partners, saying:

> We are ready, by God's grace, to face the strong antipathy in a building not fire proof . . . for we dare to say with Joshua and Caleb, "The land, which we passed through to search it, is an exceedingly good land." We look for the day, not far away, when the Lord from among this people shall join the army of the Lord, and bear testimony to His Name and to His great salvation.[8]

That was a prophecy if we've ever heard one.

Will every ministry see such incredible fruit if the partners persevere? There are plenty of church planters who've spent

---

[8] Carson, *Memoirs of an Ordinary Pastor*, 160.

decades trying to cultivate hard soil in places such as Japan and the Middle East, and they're not counting on seeing that promise fulfilled in their own lifetimes. But they keep persevering, knowing that "this benefits you" (2 Cor. 8:10) to finish the work you started. This is so not just because the road to hell is paved with good intentions, but because they know that "whoever sows bountifully will also reap bountifully" (9:6). God rewards those who persevere in their sacrificial generosity, as we'll see in the next chapter.

Walk in the fear of the Lord and in the comfort of the Holy Spirit.

Questions for Discussion:

1. What challenges and obstacles has your ministry faced so far? Slow progress? Transience? Other priorities? Differences in ministry style? Flakiness? Opposition?
2. Which heart-level diseases do you see in yourself? Externalism? Man-fearing? Despair? Impatience? How have you seen God overcome them? What does he still need to overcome?
3. Which stage are you at in collaborative ministry—forming, storming, norming, or performing? What might be holding you back from progressing to the next stage?

6

Giving and Receiving

Interdependence in Partnership

> *I do not mean that others should be eased
> and you burdened, but that as a matter of
> fairness your abundance at the present time
> should supply their need, so that their abun-
> dance may supply your need, that there may
> be fairness.*
>
> 2 CORINTHIANS 8:13–14

Matthew grew up in an idyllic Scottish village by the sea. Mez grew up in institutions in Ireland, moving from foster home to children's home to prison. No, this isn't the opening to a Charles Dickens story.

Matthew grew up trying to avoid the Mezes of the world. Mez grew up trying to steal from the Matthews of the world. But God intervened to bring these two men to Christ and, ultimately, to an unlikely partnership.

Mez had replanted a dying church in the poorest community in Scotland, called Niddrie Community Church (it sounds better with a Scottish accent). The church is located in the middle of the worst "scheme" (low-income housing project) in Edinburgh, a community plagued by drugs and prostitution. But the congregation was composed of middle-class Christians who commuted in for Sunday services and left as soon as the benediction was given. Completely isolated from the neighborhood, Niddrie was regularly firebombed by antagonistic residents.

On his first night at the church, Mez was pulled over and arrested by the police, who couldn't believe a thuggish-looking guy like him would be driving a nice car registered to a gentleman named Rev. Mez McConnell. By God's sense of humor, Mez's arrest gave him immediate street cred with his new neighbors. The church started to fill with unbelievers from the scheme, and it quickly became a vibrant hub of community life. Many people were redeemed and radically transformed by Christ. The difference between their old lives and their new was as stark as black and white.

Matthew Spandler-Davidson had moved to America and planted a church in rural Kentucky called Bardstown Christian Fellowship (he says it sounds better with a redneck accent). He had a deep desire to return to Scotland to plant churches, but never felt released by God to leave his church in Kentucky. Then, at a pastors' conference, he met Mez. Hearing about the incredible things God was doing in the schemes, Matthew saw a way to fulfill his dream and God's calling: form a partnership between the two churches.

Niddrie Community Church desperately needed funds and full-time workers to fulfill its vision to plant gospel churches across the schemes of Scotland. Reaching the residents of the schemes requires endless hours of intense personal counseling.

So Bardstown Christian Fellowship began to recruit and send trained workers for long-term ministry at Niddrie.

The partnership's vision quickly began to expand. The partner churches asked, What would it take to plant or replant gospel-driven churches in the twenty neediest schemes in Scotland? The answer: a highly trained church planter and five full-time workers for each scheme, along with the financial resources to sustain them.

This was far beyond the capacity of two churches, so Matthew and Mez launched a ministry called 20 Schemes and got to work finding additional partners. More churches soon signed on. Each church invests in one scheme church plant, sending money, long-term workers, and short-term teams. The church knows that if it doesn't follow through on its commitments, a church on the other side of the ocean might not be planted or revitalized.

But this isn't just about giving. The American churches feel that they are receiving as much as they give. After sending its first team, Bardstown Christian saw short-term missionaries come back from Scotland better equipped to reach the same kind of people they met in the schemes. Alcoholics and drug addicts started showing up at their Sunday services. Broken people with messy lives soon met Jesus through a group of Christians who, just a few years before, would have been very uncomfortable even talking to them. Matthew explained, "Making disciples in the schemes of Scotland helps us make disciples in rural Kentucky." These are disciples the church never would have made before.

As this example clearly shows, kingdom partnerships are interdependent.

Interdependence between Corinth and Jerusalem

When Paul challenged the Corinthians to send a generous contribution to Jerusalem, he didn't expect it to be a one-way street:

> As a matter of fairness your abundance at the present time should supply their need, so that their abundance may supply your need,

> that there may be fairness. As it is written, "Whoever gathered much had nothing left over, and whoever gathered little had no lack." (2 Cor. 8:13–15)

The Greek word translated as "fairness" is used in only one other place in the New Testament, when Paul commanded masters to treat each of their slaves justly and fairly (Col. 4:1). It refers to an equal measure. This means that whatever the Corinthians sent to Jerusalem, they could expect to receive back.

So are we talking about some kind of primitive insurance scheme here? Were the Corinthians saying, "We'll support you guys during this famine, but we expect you to send some cash to us when the next hundred-year storm comes our way"? Not likely. Most scholars agree with Scott Hafemann, who says: "Paul is probably referring to the Gentiles' present contribution to Israel as an expression of their spiritual fellowship and identity and to Israel's ongoing spiritual 'contribution' to the Gentiles as part of the eschatological redemption of the world. . . . The Gentiles can support the Jews financially, while the Jews can support the Gentiles with leadership and the ministry of the gospel."[1]

It's also important to recognize that this wasn't just an exchange between human parties. Paul made that clear when he referred to God's provision for the Israelites in the wilderness, quoting Exodus 16: "The people of Israel . . . gathered [the manna], some more, some less. But when they measured it . . . whoever gathered much had nothing left over, and whoever gathered little had no lack" (vv. 17–18). As God took the Israelites to the Promised Land, he miraculously made sure that each person had exactly what he needed to feed his family every day—no more, no less.

In the same way, God ensures that every church receives exactly what it needs, whether those needs are material, spiri-

---

[1] Scott J. Hafemann, 2 Corinthians, NIV Application Commentary (Grand Rapids: Zondervan, 2000), 340.

tual, or practical. And he often uses other churches as conduits of his blessing. All of us receive *something* in partnership,

What We Receive through Partnership

If we go into any ministry without hoping to receive something, we're either arrogantly proud ("What could we *ever* gain from those guys?") or arrogantly humble ("It's more blessed to give than receive, so we never want to receive *anything*"). We need to remember that engaging with the body of Christ involves engaging with Christ himself, and Jesus said he came not to be served but to serve. That means you can only come to him (and therefore his body) expecting to receive!

Peter, like many of us, had a hard time being a receiver. When Jesus wanted to wash his feet, he angrily refused: "You shall never wash my feet!" (John 13:8). In the original Greek, it's even more insistent: "By no means will you wash my feet forever!"

Why was Peter so dogmatic? Was he just embarrassed about his ugly feet, which were probably black and blue from walking miles every day, missing toenails from frequent toe-stubbings in sandals, and covered in fungi for which there were no medicines?

More likely, Peter didn't want to recognize his ongoing need. Jesus said to him, "The one who has bathed does not need to wash, except for his feet, but is completely clean" (John 13:10). He was already completely clean and justified by Christ, but he didn't want to admit that he still needed regular foot-washings: more mercy, grace, and power from Jesus every day.

Paul, who had been similarly self-sufficient before Jesus struck him blind and dependent on the road to Damascus, confronted the kind of prideful independence that can plague us all:

> By the grace given to me I say to everyone among you not to think of himself more highly than he ought to think, but to think with sober judgment, each according to the measure of faith that God has assigned. (Rom. 12:3)

He said this "sober judgment" should lead us to recognize areas of deficiency in ourselves where other parts of the body can come to our aid, since we are "individually members one of another" (Rom 12:5).

This means that there are many things you and your church might receive from the other members of Christ's body:

Stronger gospel fellowship. Fellowship between church leaders often leads to kingdom partnerships, and engaging in ministry together can help to unite leaders even more, especially when those leaders are American men. Many of us get uncomfortable sitting across a table from one another, awkwardly trying to come up with things to talk about. That's why they hang flat-screen TVs wherever men gather. We're desperate to look at anything but one another. We'd much rather be standing shoulder to shoulder, *doing* stuff together.

Take our little group of pastors. When the Kairos Project partnership launched, we had been meeting for years, and always enjoyed our time together. But beyond those four or five hours in a conference room every few months, we never really seriously engaged with one another. Then we started strategizing together, traveling together, teaching together, praying together, venturing through jungles together, and even riding a few elephants together. We'd had some semblance of fellowship before, but we weren't truly a band of brothers until we were in the trenches together. Now we support one another, challenge one another, and fight fiercely for one another all the time. And that intense bond has expanded to include pastors on the other side of the ocean.

For leaders in small churches, this kind of committed fellowship can be a lifesaver. I've worked on a church staff of more than a hundred and I've worked by myself in a church plant where the church office was my kitchen table. I know how lonely it can be to minister in a small congregation where everyone else is busy all day. Working in partnership with leaders from other churches kept me sane!

Encouragement, inspiration, and refreshment. When our little group of pastors first arrived in Southeast Asia, we met a dynamic young church planter and his wife, who had just given birth to their first son. They had named him "Kairos," believing that he was born at God's appointed time to bring transformation to their overwhelmingly anti-Christian country. They believed this gospel spark could spread throughout Southeast Asia, a region of more than six hundred million people. Coming from our humble churches on our little islands in the most geographically isolated archipelago in the world, this kind of bold faith electrified us. That's how we got the name for our partnership, the Kairos Project. We came to believe it was God's appointed time to use us *all* for kingdom-advancing ministry.

When you work together in kingdom partnership, old and tired churches are recharged by the energy of amped-up younger churches. Young and restless live-wire churches are grounded by the wisdom of established churches. And all of our churches are refreshed as we begin to stop looking so much at *ourselves.* C. S. Lewis's description of a joyfully humble man could also describe a joyfully humble church engaged in selfless partnership: "All you will think about him is that he seemed a cheerful, intelligent chap who took a real interest in what you said to him. If you do dislike him it will be because you feel a little envious of anyone who seems to enjoy life so easily. He will not be thinking about humility: he will not be thinking about himself at all."[2]

Spiritual and practical sharpening. Let's face it, every church is strange in some way. If we lived in a perfect world, each of our churches would have a wonderful diversity of gifts, strengths, and personalities, with a balance of apostles, prophets, evangelists, shepherds, and teachers (Eph. 4:11), but that almost never happens. Instead, each church tends to keep reproducing an inbred

---

[2] C. S. Lewis, *Mere Christianity* (New York: HarperCollins, 2001), 128.

family of socially awkward theological nerds (teachers), painfully culturally relevant trendsters (evangelists), or bleeding-heart lovers of every man, beast, plant, and insect (shepherds). And the more isolated we are, the more strange we get.

Working together with other churches helps make us less strange. When you serve alongside a church that's more evangelistically passionate and fruitful, you are forced to examine your own church's low number of conversions. You start praying for God to give you greater love and boldness with the lost people he's put in your sphere of influence. When you work with a church that has more well-thought-through theological foundations for everything it does, you might be challenged to confront an overly pragmatic bent in your own church. You start going back to the Bible to figure out why you do what you do, and you change what you do when you discover that it contradicts Scripture.

Greater passion for other areas of ministry. Enthusiasm grows in your church for current and potential ministries that have nothing to do with the partnership! Like Bardstown Christian Fellowship discovered, when people start to see tangible ways God is working *out there*, they tend to gain a greater vision for what he can do *right here*. This translates into more new leaders, more committed workers, and more generous giving.

One couple in our church who became involved in our Southeast Asia ministry partnership sensed God leading them to pray more for the ministry. They started gathering people in the church to pray, but their prayers quickly expanded beyond Asia. At these regular prayer meetings, dozens of people now gather to pray for our leaders, our worship services, our community groups, our children's ministry, our neighborhoods, our islands, and our world.

Tangible assistance. If you are part of a church that's small in numbers but big in vision, kingdom partnership may be the way God plans to provide the resources you need to fulfill the mission he's given you. That's how Niddrie Community Church started to reach the schemes of Scotland, and it's also how our church-based theological training program was born. A few years after our church was planted, we found ourselves with an increasing number of strong young men who sensed God leading them to plant churches or revitalize dying churches. We wanted to send them out, but they desperately needed training. As the sole staff member (and even the sole elder!) in our church at that time, there was no way I could train them all effectively by myself. So God provided wise, experienced, like-minded pastors from other churches to help. He also provided much-needed funds from other churches that allowed us to bring on a full-time director, Chris, to lead our fast-growing partnership.

Interdependence can be lifesaving. In one international church-planting partnership, a partner pastor in a dangerous nation was tragically killed by religious extremists. His wife and unborn child were targeted next. They needed to escape the country quickly. Word spread in the partnership, and one small church had a pilot with access to a private jet who offered to fly seventy-five hundred miles from America to pick them up. Praise God, they were able to reach safety through the help of partner churches even without the plane.

God designed his body to be wonderfully interdependent. We can always expect to receive as much as we give *and more*, because we're receiving directly from Christ himself. Hudson Taylor, who experienced arrests, insults, slander, and poverty during his ministry in China, was famous for saying, "I never made a sacrifice." His son later confirmed the heartfelt sentiment behind that statement, saying, "What he said was true, for the compensations were so real and lasting that he came to see that giving up is inevitably receiving when one is dealing heart to heart with God."[3]

---

[3] Howard and Geraldine Taylor, *Hudson Taylor's Spiritual Secret*, Moody Classics (Chicago: Moody, 2009), 31.

Still, there are destructive attitudes that can quickly kill this kind of joyful interdependence in the body of Christ.

The Enemies of Interdependence

There are parts of your physical body that you love to show off to the world, such as your pearly white teeth or your gorgeous brown eyes. Then there are parts that no one but your doctor should ever see. These parts are vital to your health and everyday life, but they aren't very impressive. Paul imagined a conversation between these different body parts:

> If the foot should say, "Because I am not a hand, I do not belong to the body," that would not make it any less a part of the body. And if the ear should say, "Because I am not an eye, I do not belong to the body," that would not make it any less a part of the body. If the whole body were an eye, where would be the sense of hearing? If the whole body were an ear, where would be the sense of smell? (1 Cor. 12:15–17)

He was talking about the members of a local church, where some people feel as if they don't match up to the giftedness, talent, and attractiveness of some others. These "feet people" compare themselves to the "eye people" and feel inferior. And the same dynamic can exist in a kingdom partnership. There are some "feet churches" that have fewer people, less money, and less-obvious giftedness. They look enviously at the "eye churches," with their armies of workers, endless resources, and charismatic leaders. They start to feel inferior and useless. In their insecurity, they're tempted to step aside and let the big dogs take over.

But Paul would have none of that. "Stop with the pity party!" he would say to them. "Just because your role isn't as glamorous doesn't mean it's not just as vitally needed!"

Confronting an Attitude of Inferiority and Uselessness

"If the whole body were an eye, where would be the sense of hearing?" Paul asked. The "eye churches" may be doing great things, but they often overlook crucially important aspects of kingdom ministry. If you're in a large, established church with many paid ministry staff workers, you might not understand what it's like for a single pastor to carry the burden of leading an entire church by himself. So in a church-planting partnership, when you're setting the bar for what you hope to see church planters accomplish in their new little churches, you need the input of smaller-church pastors who know what's realistic and what's not.

We need one another desperately. Some of our churches are beautiful brown eyes, while some are smelly armpits that do nothing but sweat and keep the body from overheating. And that's the way the Holy Spirit designed us: "As it is, God arranged the members in the body, each one of them, as he chose" (1 Cor. 12:18). If you don't like the way God designed your church and its place in the kingdom, you're implicitly saying you don't think God knows what he's doing. He deliberately designed us to be interdependent, not to feel threatened by leaders and churches that have gifts and blessings from God that seem better than ours.

Sometimes "feet leaders" know they're not equipped to be "eye leaders," but they refuse to be satisfied with a less-prominent role. They can't accept the way God has designed them and their churches. Paul addressed this problem as well:

> The parts of the body that seem to be weaker are indispensable, and on those parts of the body that we think less honorable we bestow the greater honor, and our unpresentable parts are treated with greater modesty, which our more presentable parts do not require. But God has so composed the body, giving greater honor to the part that lacked it. (1 Cor. 12:22–24)

Unpresentable parts are to be treated with greater modesty. Paul was speaking directly to "feet leaders" and "feet churches" that desperately crave the same kind of exposure and attention as the eyes. I have a friend who met this kind of leader in a preaching class in seminary. One day, the classmate got up to give his assigned sermon. It was awful, just excruciatingly bad, from the theology down to the delivery. The professor tried gently to tell him that, but the student angrily cut him off, saying: "No! You're wrong. I've been anointed by God to preach! He gave me the *gift* of preaching!" The professor replied flatly, "Well, if that's true, then he didn't give any of us the gift of listening."

Paul was speaking directly to that prideful preacher and thousands more like him, saying: "Be happy with the gifts the Holy Spirit has given you! Don't demand to be put in a prominent place like the leaders and churches that have different gifts. Our unpresentable parts need greater modesty!" This is because there's honor in modesty. There's honor in silent, invisible service to the kingdom. If you think the only way you can advance the kingdom is with a microphone in your hand, then you don't understand the kind of kingdom Jesus is building.

Confronting an Attitude of Superiority and Arrogance

Paul also had a few words to say to the guys who *should be* holding the microphone:

> If all were a single member, where would the body be? As it is, there are many parts, yet one body. The eye cannot say to the hand, "I have no need of you," nor again the head to the feet, "I have no need of you." (1 Cor. 12:19–21)

So now we're talking about the "eye churches" with big crowds, overflowing offering plates, and charismatic leaders. They look at the less-gifted leaders and less-prominent churches and say, "Uhhhh . . . what is it exactly you do around here, again?" They start to marginalize the "feet churches," slowly and subconsciously at first. Before long, the "feet churches" come to realize they have no significant role in the ministry at all.

To Paul, that kind of maneuver would be laughably self-defeating. "What good would your eyes be without hands and feet?" he asked. Such eyes would be stuck on the sofa watching city council meetings on public-access TV all day, unable to walk away or change the channel!

Paul was pointing out the ridiculousness of division in the body of Christ. When different parts of the same body declare war on each other, who wins? When the hand decides to pick up a gun and shoot the foot, who wins? All the parts lose! We're interdependent. We need one another. It doesn't matter whether our churches are flashy and high-powered or slow, silent, and invisible. God uses us all—eyes, feet, and sweaty armpits—to advance his kingdom *together*.

The Limits of Interdependence

Feet are immediately utilitarian: you use them to get one step ahead. Eyes might seem to be more passive: they observe and influence. Both are needed, but "feet churches" can be tempted to complain that "eye churches" are not utilitarian enough: "Why are you wasting your time staring off into the distance? There's *work* to do!"

There is always more to do in partnership. There is always more money we could give away, more people we could send, and more projects we could undertake. Oskar Schindler expressed this kind of anxiety at the end of the movie *Schindler's List*, distressed over all the things he had kept for himself that could have bought the lives of more Jews who died in the concentration camps: "This car. . . . Why did I keep the car? Ten people, right there, ten more I could've got." There's always more we can do.

But God never intended us to live in a continual state of low-level guilt over the many things we could be doing and aren't. Paul made that clear to the Corinthians:

> If the readiness is there, it is acceptable according to what a person has, not according to what he does not have. For I do not mean that others should be eased and you burdened. (2 Cor. 8:12–13)

In other words, the best way for a richer church to help a poorer church isn't necessarily for the rich church to become poor, giving away all its money the minute it is dropped in the offering plate. God may grant particular grace to some churches to give beyond their means, as he did for the Macedonians. But he never *demands* that we harm ourselves in order to bless others.

On one trip to Southeast Asia, our group of pastors was meeting with the leader of a large church. He took us to a plot of land the church had recently purchased, telling us that it was actively seeking financial partners to help build a nice five thousand-seat auditorium. We all looked around at one another, struggling to contain our snickers. With the astronomical price of real estate in our city, none of our churches could afford buildings of their own. We were all meeting in old, run-down school cafeterias and community centers that could fit no more than 250. Short of a Macedonian miracle, we didn't think the people of our congregations would be whipping out their checkbooks anytime soon to pay for another church's plush theater seating while they themselves sat on rickety metal folding chairs.

Sowing Bountifully

We shouldn't feel pressure to kill ourselves for the sake of others, but we should also remember that "whoever sows sparingly will also reap sparingly, and whoever sows bountifully will also reap bountifully" (2 Cor. 9:6). If you're a farmer and you don't sow many seeds, you're not going to have many crops. It's a simple equation.

But in Paul's culture (as in much of the developing world today), a farmer couldn't just go down to the feed store and pick up a bag of seed. You had to take it from the previous year's harvest. Once you scattered your seed, it was all gone. You couldn't get more. So when you went out to sow your seed, it was a major act of faith.

If you don't throw all your seed out on the ground, you won't have food to eat, but you'll still have the seed. It won't do you much good when you die of starvation, but at least you'll still have it. If you do throw out that seed and it doesn't grow, you won't have food to eat *and* you won't have any seed. So with every toss of your arm, you're making yourself more and more dependent on God. He's got to come through and make this seed grow, or else you'll die! *And that's exactly where he wants you.*

It's common sense that you'll have more if you keep more, but Paul believed the opposite: you'll have more if you *give more.* When you and your church sow bountifully, you'll reap bountifully.

The people of Bardstown Christian Fellowship saw this first-hand. They sowed bountiful amounts of money, leaders, and servants in Scotland. And they reaped bountiful numbers of new believers in their own neighborhood.

Get ready to receive.

Questions for Discussion:

1. What have you already received through partnership? Expanded gospel fellowship? Encouragement, inspiration, and refreshment? Spiritual and practical sharpening? Greater passion for other areas of ministry? Tangible assistance?

2. What do you hope to receive more of?

3. Which enemies of interdependence need to be confronted in your ministry? Attitudes of inferiority and uselessness? Attitudes of superiority and arrogance?

7

Expanding Ownership

Building Engagement, Enthusiasm,
and Dedication

Each one must give as he has decided in his
heart, not reluctantly or under compulsion,
for God loves a cheerful giver.

2 Corinthians 9:7

The live TV coverage was horrifying.

Terrorized students streamed out of the school. A bloodstained boy struggled to escape through a second-story window. The heavily armed SWAT team waited impatiently at the school entrance while shots continued to ring out inside. Soon, two yearbook pictures were flashed on the screen as the final death toll was announced. Two lonely, outcast teenage boys had killed twelve students and one teacher in Columbine High School before finally killing themselves.

In the previous two years, students and teachers across the United States had been slaughtered in seven different school shootings in small cities and towns. These senseless tragedies all took place in the kinds of neighborhoods people moved to because they felt safe. None of the killers were drug dealers or convicted felons. All but one were quiet, lonely teenage boys. The entire nation intuitively felt the same thing: this was an epidemic.

A pastor named Jay Jarman came to the same conclusion as he watched the images on TV. He wondered whether anything could be done to prevent it from happening in his town. "How can we reach these kids?" Jay asked himself. He quickly realized it was probably too late by the time they were teenagers. Troubled children needed to be loved and mentored by caring adults while they were still in elementary school.

Jay met with the principal of a local elementary school, who immediately loved the idea. She could identify a handful of the school's loneliest kids off the top of her head. Jay recruited, trained, and background-checked volunteers from his church, who began meeting with kids at the school for an hour each week. It was often difficult. Progress was slow. But many of these relationships blossomed into lifelong friendships. Some of the kids put their trust in Jesus.

Still, this was just scratching the surface. There were hundreds of schools in Jay's city, far too many for one church to even think about reaching. So he was sent out by the leaders of his church to share the vision with more churches. He launched an organization called Common Grace, which connects neighborhood churches with nearby public elementary schools, trains and vets their volunteer mentors, and facilitates regular activities for mentors to enjoy with their kids.

When a church partners with an elementary school, a long-term relationship is launched. Mentors become teammates alongside the teachers and administrators, enmeshed in the life of the school. The pastor might be called in to help counsel students in crisis, teach parenting workshops, or even pray before faculty meetings (don't tell the ACLU)! Others from the church might volunteer for cleaning and maintenance projects at the school. The entire church body soon starts to develop strong feelings of responsibility for the welfare of the school and the families in the surrounding neighborhood.

A sense of ownership makes all the difference.

The Importance of Ownership

Tech companies give out stock options to their best employees, and law firms invite high-performing associates to become equity partners. They know how crucial it is for their people to have a vested interest in the organization. When you've got "skin in the game," when the company's bottom line affects *your* bottom line, you're much more likely to sacrifice your time, energy, and enthusiasm to ensure everyone's success.

It's clear from Scripture that Jesus is the one who actually owns everything: "All things were created through him and for him. And he is before all things, and in him all things hold together" (Col. 1:16–17). As Abraham Kuyper said so well, "There is not a square inch in the whole domain of our human existence over which Christ, who is Sovereign over all, does not cry, Mine!"[1] But if we hope to lead like the Good Shepherd, we will feel the same weight of responsibility for the flocks entrusted to us that Jesus felt. Remember what he said?

> I am the good shepherd. The good shepherd lays down his life for the sheep. He who is a hired hand and not a shepherd, who does not own the sheep, sees the wolf coming and leaves the sheep and flees, and the wolf snatches them and scatters them.

---

[1] Abraham Kuyper, "Sphere Sovereignty," in *Abraham Kuyper: A Centennial Reader*, ed. James D. Bratt (Grand Rapids: Eerdmans, 1998), 488.

He flees because he is a hired hand and cares nothing for the sheep. (John 10:11–13)

A shepherd feels a strong sense of obligation to the flock. A hired hand just wants to use the flock for his own benefit. A shepherd is willing to lay down his life for the flock. A hired hand runs away when things get tough. He has no vested interest in the flock, only in his own welfare.

Peter, who was personally exhorted by the Good Shepherd to shepherd his sheep, passed along the same challenge to other leaders in the flock:

> Shepherd the flock of God that is among you, exercising oversight, not under compulsion, but willingly, as God would have you; not for shameful gain, but eagerly; not domineering over those in your charge, but being examples to the flock. (1 Peter 5:2–3)

Hired hands serve under compulsion, work for shameful gain, and are impatiently domineering. But shepherds feel a personal stewardship for the people and programs under their care. They exercise oversight willingly and joyfully, as eager examples of Christlike concern. No church can survive and thrive without true shepherds. Neither can any kingdom partnership.

Building a Sense of Ownership

In every partnership, there comes a time when you need to know who will lay down their lives and who won't; who will stand firm even when the wolves start to bare their teeth and who will run away at the first sign of trouble. The good news is, it's possible for God to turn hired hands into shepherds.

The Corinthian church could have served as the *very definition* of a bunch of hired hands. They were always running away! But as Paul patiently encouraged them toward full participation in the Jerusalem collection partnership, he showed us some of the strategies that can help us build a Christlike sense of ownership in a shared ministry.

1. Avoid an Atmosphere of Pressure and Guilt

Paul went to great lengths to avoid any kind of compulsion as he encouraged the Corinthian church to engage fully in the partnership:

> I thought it necessary to urge the brothers to go on ahead to you and arrange in advance for the gift you have promised, so that it may be ready as a willing gift, not as an exaction. The point is this: whoever sows sparingly will also reap sparingly, and whoever sows bountifully will also reap bountifully. Each one must give as he has decided in his heart, not reluctantly or under compulsion, for God loves a cheerful giver. (2 Cor. 9:5–7)

Paul didn't want it to seem as if he were shaking down the people in the church in Corinth, so he sent three other trusted partners ahead who could help them work out what their participation would look like. He knew what kind of pressure the presence of an apostle of Jesus Christ would bring, and he didn't want the Corinthians to feel that he was just showing up out of the blue and saying, "Show me the money!" So instead of rushing them into a hasty decision, Paul gave them plenty of time to think and pray about their involvement.

You can be sure he was tempted to do the opposite. The Christians in Jerusalem were suffering and dying every day. The need was urgent, but Paul still didn't want to pressure the Corinthians into giving before they were ready.

When you see a crying need along with a wide-open opportunity to respond, it's easy to believe that you'll miss the boat unless you act quickly and decisively. Go big and go now, or go home! Sure enough, this kind of urgency can quickly inspire others to climb on board.

But this approach can also backfire, leading people to give "sparingly," as Paul described. Giving sparingly means holding something back. Christians who feel pressured into giving often give this way. "I'll give a tithe," they say to themselves, "but that's 10 percent of my pay *after taxes*, and that doesn't include my Christmas bonus or my tax refund. I need that for my vacation."

Churches can fall into the same kind of sparing participation as they enter into partnership. When we feel pressured into sacrificial generosity, it's too easy for us to become like Ananias and Sapphira, giving the bare minimum necessary to look good rather than giving whatever it takes to glorify God and advance his kingdom.

Ananias and Sapphira watched with eyes wide open as the church in Jerusalem cared for the needy among them: "As many as were owners of lands or houses sold them and brought the proceeds of what was sold and laid it at the apostles' feet, and it was distributed to each as any had need" (Acts 4:34–35). Their jaws dropped as Barnabas, a wealthy landowner, sold his property and laid every cent of the money at the apostles' feet (vv. 36–37).

Also being wealthy landowners, Ananias and Sapphira started feeling pressure to be just as generous as Barnabas. They had an investment property they had been planning to sell, but there was something else they wanted to do with the profits. Maybe they hoped to buy a new sailboat. They wanted the honor and respect they would gain if they gave a big gift to the church, but they really wanted the sailboat too. So they tried to have their cake and eat it too:

> Ananias, with his wife Sapphira, sold a piece of property, and with his wife's knowledge he kept back for himself some of the proceeds and brought only a part of it and laid it at the apostles' feet. (5:1–2)

Peter saw right through this nakedly ambitious scheme:

> Peter said, "Ananias, why has Satan filled your heart to lie to the Holy Spirit and to keep back for yourself part of the proceeds

of the land? While it remained unsold, did it not remain your own? And after it was sold, was it not at your disposal? Why is it that you have contrived this deed in your heart?" (vv. 3–4)

In other words: "Who would have complained if you had given just half of what you made from the property and told us the truth, Ananias? The sin wasn't in what you held back, the sin was in your desire to look more generous than you really are." As John Calvin said, Ananias lied because he honored the apostles' feet more than God's eyes.[2]

In the Sermon on the Mount, Jesus warned, "Beware of practicing your righteousness before other people in order to be seen by them" (Matt. 6:1). The *only* reason Ananias and Sapphira acted righteous was to be seen. Jesus said, "When you give to the needy, do not let your left hand know what your right hand is doing, so that your giving may be in secret" (vv. 3–4). Ananias and Sapphira made absolutely sure it wasn't a secret to anyone how much they were giving. Jesus said, "Do not lay up for yourselves treasures on earth, where moth and rust destroy and where thieves break in and steal, but lay up for yourselves treasures in heaven. . . . For where your treasure is, there your heart will be also" (vv. 19–21). Ananias and Sapphira treasured the prestige of man more than they treasured God and his kingdom.

Leaders and churches who feel guilt-tripped into giving often give only what it takes to burnish their image and get you off their back. Instead, we want to inspire unsparing generosity. And that happens only as we model it ourselves as a normal part of everyday life, which is what Jesus meant when he said we should give so that our left hand doesn't know what our right hand is doing (Matt. 6:3).

On the night I proposed to my wife, more than twenty years ago, I took her out for the nicest dinner either of us had ever

[2] John Calvin, *Commentary on Acts*, vol. 1, Christian Classics Ethereal Library online edition, www.ccel.org/ccel/calvin/calcom36.xii.i.html (accessed Jan. 9, 2013).

eaten. I said: "Order anything you want, baby. We're sparing no expense tonight!" There was nothing on the menu I was holding back from her. She didn't think twice; she ordered the lobster, the priciest item she could find. I couldn't have been happier. Ever since, we've been in good-natured competition to see who can be more generous toward the other. One year, a few days before Father's Day, I drove home from work to find a motorcycle sitting in my carport with a big red bow on top. Unsparingness is contagious.

2. Cultivate an Atmosphere of Delight in Duty

Unsparing generosity is birthed out of joy. We want churches to be joyfully and enthusiastically engaged because this builds a sense of ownership. Paul said to the Corinthians:

> God loves a cheerful giver. And God is able to make all grace abound to you, so that having all sufficiency in all things at all times, you may abound in every good work. As it is written, "He has distributed freely, he has given to the poor; his righteousness endures forever." (2 Cor. 9:7–9)

"God loves a cheerful giver." Most of us have heard more than a few sermons that use this verse as the motivation for giving our weekly offerings, and that's certainly a legitimate application. But did you ever notice that this favorite verse of pastors everywhere is used specifically to encourage generosity in a kingdom partnership?

Paul described the cheerful giving of the Jerusalem collection partner churches another way: "They were pleased to do it, and indeed they owe it to them" (Rom. 15:27). They were pleased to give, and at the same time, they owed it. As John Piper observes: "There is no necessary conflict between duty and delight. It is possible to love doing what you ought to do. Indeed, you *should* pursue that joy in your life."[3] So in our partnerships, we need to cultivate an atmosphere of both delight *and* duty.

Paul said the Corinthians' cheerful giving was motivated by God's "inexpressible gift" of his Son (2 Cor. 9:15). So good works—works that please God and reflect obedience to him—include both our actions and our motivations for those actions, ultimately rooted in the gospel itself.

The problem is that, due to our sinful hearts, our delight and duty don't always correspond. You could joyfully avoid taxes for a few decades and buy yourself a new Bugatti Veyron with the money you save. You could delightfully gun your new supercar up to 200 miles per hour on the freeway. But your unsuppressed joy through it all wouldn't keep you out of prison for tax evasion and reckless endangerment. Regardless of our feelings, there are certain things we always need to do, such as paying taxes, driving the speed limit, and, yes, giving generously. Whether the Corinthians wanted to or not, it was their duty to contribute to the partnership. They had made a commitment, and they were obligated to keep their word.

Still, the mere act of contributing wasn't enough to change the Corinthians from hired hands to Christlike shepherds. This is one of those beautiful tensions you see often in the Bible: if they did it only out of duty, they would not actually be fulfilling their duty! They would show they were not trusting God's abundant grace to them.

So as we seek to help our partners grab hold of the mission God's given us and really own it, we need to work hard to cultivate an atmosphere of dutiful delight. But how do we do this?

Paul did it by emphasizing the incredible grace of God as the source of our joy in ministry. He reminded the Corinthians that "God is able to make all grace abound to you, so that having all

---

[3] John Piper, "Joy + Debt = A Two-Thousand-Mile Detour to Jerusalem," Desiring God blog post, Sept. 10, 2006, www.desiringgod.org/resource-library/sermons/joydebt-a-two-thousand-mile-detour-to-jerusalem (accessed Feb. 21, 2014).

sufficiency in all things at all times, you may abound in every good work" (v. 8). There are a lot of unconditional statements in there: *all* grace . . . *all* sufficiency . . . in *all* things . . . at *all* times . . . for *every* good work. In other words, God gives you everything you need to do everything he asks. This means that, as David Garland puts it, "Reluctance to sow generously reflects a refusal to trust that God is all sufficient and all gracious."[4]

In kingdom partnerships, this principle plays itself out as churches learn to contribute joyfully to kingdom-expanding work with the expectation that God will supply all of the resources they need. A sense of ownership in a kingdom partnership comes from recognizing and grabbing hold of God's overflowing grace.

3. Cultivate an Atmosphere of Mutual Praise
When you are focused relentlessly on God's grace, you are led naturally to worship. You see the way God is at work in other churches, and you cannot keep from celebrating it. Likewise, you fall over yourself to point out the great things you see in others.

Paul did this with, of all people, the Corinthian church. While he repeatedly praised the generous Macedonians to the Corinthians, it's surprising to see that he also did the reverse:

> It is superfluous for me to write to you about the ministry for the saints, for I know your readiness, of which I boast about you to the people of Macedonia, saying that Achaia [i.e., Corinth] has been ready since last year. And your zeal has stirred up most of them. (2 Cor. 9:1–2)

Paul was willing to put his own reputation on the line for the sake of the rebellious, licentious, and litigious Corinthians by boasting to the Macedonians about them. You can imagine how *that* conversation probably went down:

---

[4] David Garland, *2 Corinthians*, New American Commentary, vol. 29 (Nashville: Broadman & Holman, 1999), 407.

"Hey, did you hear that the Corinthians are joining the partnership? They're going to send a big gift to Jerusalem!"

"Hold on. Did you just say 'the *Corinthians*'? The guys who get plastered at church potlucks, sleep with their stepmothers, and sue each other's pants off? *Those* guys? Are you kidding me?"

"Yeah, I know, but they *are* the church of God that is in Corinth, sanctified in Christ Jesus, called to be saints together with all those who in every place call upon the name of our Lord Jesus Christ."

"Ohhh-kaaayyy, Paul. Whatever you say, man."

Regardless of the Corinthians' many shortcomings, Paul praised them because of the grace of God among them. If he could do that, surely you can find reasons to praise the church whose theology is a little weak or the leader who keeps flaking out on his commitments. Be willing to stick your neck out a little bit for the churches you are partnered with and boast about them to others.

One of the most effective ways to do this is to regularly praise other churches and pastors in public. In your church services, pray for other churches and praise God for the way he is working in them. Hearing how God is at work in other churches will get your church excited about working with them. And as the other churches hear about this, they'll be more excited about working with you.

When you meet with your partners, take time in every meeting to share how God has been at work in your churches. Be quick to point out evidences of God's grace, both to them and to others. Be active in praying for one another regularly. Let other leaders and churches run with ideas and initiatives that might not be particularly exciting to you, but that still contribute to the overall mission of the partnership. Kill your pride, and don't be surprised when an idea that you thought would never work turns out to be just the thing your ministry needed. As you and your partners practice these things, you will soon gain a greater appreciation for one another, leading to a greater sense of ownership for the ministry and a greater commitment to work together to advance God's kingdom.

4. Cultivate an Atmosphere of Openness and Accountability

With the possible exception of sexual sin among leaders, there is nothing more devastating to a church—or a church partnership—than financial mismanagement. When it came to the delicate matter of money, Paul went to great lengths to be open and transparent:

> Being himself very earnest [Titus] is going to you of his own accord. With him we are sending the brother who is famous among all the churches for his preaching of the gospel. And not only that, but he has been appointed by the churches to travel with us as we carry out this act of grace that is being ministered by us, for the glory of the Lord himself and to show our good will. We take this course so that no one should blame us about this generous gift that is being administered by us, for we aim at what is honorable not only in the Lord's sight but also in the sight of man. And with them we are sending our brother whom we have often tested and found earnest in many matters, but who is now more earnest than ever because of his great confidence in you. (2 Cor. 8:17–22)

Paul didn't want to receive the money from Corinth himself. Instead, he sent three trusted leaders, who would be responsible to receive the gift and pass it along to Jerusalem. They would keep one another in check. Paul explained why this was necessary: "We take this course so that no one should blame us about this generous gift that is being administered by us" (v. 20). By his extreme caution, he was protecting himself, the Corinthians, and the suffering saints in Jerusalem.

Paul worked hard to make sure the leadership of the Jerusalem collection partnership was shared, open, and accountable. He knew that for leaders and churches to be true shepherds rather than hired hands, they needed to understand they were investing resources, people, and sweat in a partnership, not just giving to a personality.

That can be difficult to pull off in a personality-obsessed culture like that of Corinth ("I follow Paul!" "I follow Apollos!"; see 1 Cor. 1:10–17), and especially our own. We love serving and contributing in places where important, influential, and well-liked people might take notice of our great generosity and pay a little more attention to us.

I was once the guest preacher for a few months at a retirement-home chapel service. The members of the congregation had an offering basket by the pulpit, and all the money went to the preacher. After the service, each person filed past the offering basket, moving slowly in walkers and wheelchairs, while everyone else watched. They tossed in a dollar or two, maybe ten, depending on how good the preacher was. If they really got goosebumps (or, as we say in Hawaii, "chicken-skin"), you might get a twenty! After everyone had filed past, the preacher was expected to pull all the money out of the basket himself. My first Sunday there, I tried to decline politely, but it was quickly made clear to me that was not an option. So I sheepishly went up and started pulling the cash out of the basket, stuffing fistfuls of one-dollar bills into my pockets while everyone watched. I felt like I was an exotic dancer.

Paul desperately wanted to avoid a scene like that, so he didn't go to Corinth and ask them to hand over a big wad of cash to him personally. Instead, he sent three trusted partners who would be responsible to receive the offering and pass it along. They would all share authority for the resources entrusted to the partnership. Ownership and responsibility flourish where openness and transparency are cultivated.

What True Shepherds Produce

A sense of ownership is essential to any flourishing ministry. Just ask the churches of Common Grace. In a little over ten years, the ministry has expanded from a few volunteers at a single elementary school to a partnership of more than fifty churches that have ministered at just as many schools across the state. Over a thousand lonely, at-risk children have been mentored by loving uncles and aunties.

Those children include a kid named Jackson. His mentor, Ron, met him when Jackson was a second-grader who couldn't read. Ron spent an hour a week with him, trying to build trust and love. Progress was slow. Jackson didn't want to look at books, so Uncle Ron tried to teach him how to play chess. He invited Jackson to a church event, where security cameras caught Jackson starting a fire in a trash can that quickly spread to a nearby church wall. Fortunately, the fire was extinguished before too much damage was done, and God used the experience to break through to Jackson's heart. Jackson put his faith in Christ and soon began sharing the gospel with his entire family. He is now part of the middle-school ministry at Ron's church, and recently brought his unbelieving grandfather along to a church men's retreat. And he can now beat Uncle Ron at chess.

That's what God does through true shepherds. There are hundreds more stories like this, all told by mentors who would say, "This is *my* kid," and churches that would say, "This is *our* school."

True shepherds feel a sense of ownership for the ministry God has given them.

Questions for Discussion:

1. In what ways might your partnership be characterized by pressure and guilt? In what ways is it characterized by delight in duty?
2. What's one evidence of God's grace that you can see and praise in another church right now? When was the last time you did this publicly?
3. What specific steps could you take to make your ministry more open and accountable?

8

Launching a Movement

Multiplying Ministries for God's Glory

He who supplies seed to the sower and bread for food will supply and multiply your seed for sowing and increase the harvest of your righteousness. You will be enriched in every way to be generous in every way, which through us will produce thanksgiving to God.

2 Corinthians 9:10–11

When Dan Davis looked around Austin, Texas, in the mid-1980s, he didn't see many churches working together. First Baptist and Third Baptist weren't even talking to each other.

But Dan had a deep desire to see the gospel advance in Austin in ways he knew his church could not accomplish alone. So he decided to have coffee with every pastor he could find. Slowly but surely, Dan got to know dozens of pastors around Austin. And as he got to know these pastors, he also started connecting them with one another. When these pastors from different backgrounds and denominations got to know one another, they were shocked to discover that they actually liked one another! The Austin Bridge Builders Alliance (ABBA) was born.

These pastors began an annual prayer retreat, praying for their city and looking for ways to work together to bless it. At their first retreat, ten pastors committed to give an extra ten percent of their time, above and beyond what they gave to their congregations, to help launch ministry partnerships. After two short days together, they came away with *forty-one* partnership goals, including everything from caring for orphans to matching dying churches with growing congregations that needed buildings. Talk about starting with ambition!

Momentum began to build, and within a few years ABBA had helped launch dozens of church partnerships in the greater Austin area. Ministries started to multiply so rapidly that ABBA had to divide the city into nine partnership regions. Today, churches partner together within each region to launch diverse ministries, from homeless housing projects to business-as-mission initiatives. ABBA now connects more than 120 churches for ministry across Austin.

It's always easier for a church to do things on its own. It cuts out all the problems of building unity, trust, and stewardship. But the partner churches of ABBA will tell you that when you work to overcome these challenges and see partnerships start to gain momentum, the effort is worth it. And as ministry partnerships grow, they multiply. Before you know it, your small fellowship could launch dozens of overlapping ministry partnerships that fan out across the city, or even the world, to have a profound impact for the kingdom. And as these partnerships multiply, the news about them reverberates for God's glory.

Multiplied Seed

Paul said that's exactly what should happen: "He who supplies seed to the sower and bread for food will supply and *multiply your seed for sowing and increase the harvest of your righteousness.* You will be enriched in every way to be generous in every way, which through us will produce thanksgiving to God" (2 Cor. 9:10–11).

No matter what the televangelists say, Paul wasn't talking about a financial harvest for our own benefit. If you give anything so that God will multiply it back and you'll have more for yourself, you're not understanding this verse correctly. Paul said God would multiply your seed *for sowing.* We give so that God will give us *even more to give*!

This is clear when you understand the Old Testament passage Paul was drawing from:

> For as the rain and the snow come down from heaven and do not return there but water the earth, making it bring forth and sprout, giving seed to the sower and bread to the eater, so shall my word be that goes out from my mouth; it shall not return to me empty, but it shall accomplish that which I purpose, and shall succeed in the thing for which I sent it. (Isa. 55:10–11)

Paul was hinting that the Corinthians' seed would multiply through more opportunities for the Word of God to go forward. And as God's Word goes forward, it accomplishes its purpose. It succeeds. It does amazing things. More leaders are raised. More ministries are multiplied. More people become citizens of the kingdom.

Think about how the seed multiplied in the early church:

John the Baptist introduced Andrew to Jesus.
  Andrew brought Simon Peter.
    Peter preached to three thousand pilgrims in
    Jerusalem at Pentecost.
      Some of those new believers went home to
      Antioch and planted a church.
        The church of Antioch discipled and sent
        Paul and Barnabas.
          Paul went to Corinth and discipled
          Priscilla and Aquilla.
            Priscilla and Aquilla went to
            Ephesus and taught Apollos.
              Apollos went back to Corinth
              and powerfully convinced the
              Jews that Jesus was the Christ
              (Acts 18:28).
          At the same time, Paul mentored
          Timothy.
            Timothy went to Ephesus and
            entrusted what he had heard from
            Paul to faithful men who were able
            to teach others also (2 Tim. 2:2).
        Paul also discipled Titus.
          Titus planted and strengthened
          churches in every town on the
          island of Crete (Titus 1:5).

When John the Baptist sat down by himself in the wilderness for a dinner of locusts and honey, do you think he ever imagined that he would be changing the lives of Jews and Gentiles across the Roman empire in far-flung places such as Corinth, Ephesus, and Crete? Probably not. But that's the way seed works. It multiplies!

This isn't true just for multiplying disciples. It also applies to multiplying ministries. And that's what makes a movement.

Paul's Multiplying Partnerships

Paul was always looking for ways to multiply ministries. Think about the way he challenged the Roman church. First, he invited the Romans to join the Jerusalem collection partnership. While they probably weren't one of the financial partners, Paul asked the church to "strive together with me in your prayers to God on my behalf, that I may be delivered from the unbelievers in Judea, and that my service for Jerusalem may be acceptable to the saints" (Rom. 15:30–31).

He knew that he would face many dangers from both Jews and Gentiles when he delivered the gift, so he asked the Romans to contribute to the Jerusalem collection in a crucial way: intercession. Many of us view prayer as a perfunctory box to be checked before we get down to the real work of ministry, but Paul saw prayer, with and for one another, as a primary way to *do* actual ministry together. So he asked the Romans to join the Jerusalem collection partnership as hardworking prayer partners.

But his partnership plans didn't end there. After he delivered the money to Jerusalem, Paul hoped to launch a new ministry in Spain along with the Romans: "I hope to see you in passing as I go to Spain, and to be helped on my journey there by you, once I have enjoyed your company for a while" (v. 24). This was a new church-planting partnership, and Paul wanted the Romans to get in on the ground floor by helping him on his journey.

And he wasn't content to work only with the Romans. We believe Paul was also trying to recruit his old friends the Philippians (aka the Macedonians) into this new partnership. Follow us as we do a little New Testament detective work.

When he wrote the letter we now know as Philippians, Paul was in prison. Most scholars think that he was writing from Rome after he had been arrested when delivering the Jerusalem collection and sent to Caesar (see Acts 21:27ff.; 25:11–12; 27–28).

But there's a problem with this theory. In his letter, Paul said he planned to return to Philippi when he was released from prison:

"I hope therefore to send [Timothy] just as soon as I see how it will go with me, and I trust in the Lord that shortly I myself will come also" (Phil. 2:23–24). However, we just heard Paul tell the Romans that when he finally made it to Rome, he wanted to go from there to Spain. So if he was in Rome when he wrote to the Philippians, why would he backtrack to Philippi after his release? Why not push ahead to Spain, the last unevangelized region of the Mediterranean? Why take a forty-day journey in the wrong direction?[1]

It was because he wanted to recruit the Philippians into partnership again![2] They were his most faithful partners. In addition to their extreme generosity toward the saints in Jerusalem, they supported Paul's church-planting ministry: "You Philippians yourselves know that in the beginning of the gospel, when I left Macedonia, no church entered into partnership with me in giving and receiving, except you only" (Phil. 4:15). Even while he sat in prison in Rome, they still cared for him: "I have received full payment, and more. I am well supplied, having received from Epaphroditus the gifts you sent, a fragrant offering, a sacrifice acceptable and pleasing to God" (v. 18).

So *why wouldn't* Paul want to include his most faithful friends in a partnership for ministry to the most far-flung place he had ever visited? He was always looking for ways to bring people into

---

[1] For this reason (among others), scholars such as D. A. Carson and Douglas Moo have argued that there is a "strong but far from conclusive case" to be made for Ephesus as Paul's location while writing Philippians (see D. A. Carson and Douglas J. Moo, *An Introduction to the New Testament*, 2nd ed. [Grand Rapids: Zondervan, 2005], 506). But the lack of any mention of an Ephesian imprisonment in the New Testament makes this argument difficult to accept.

[2] We're proposing a novel solution here to the centuries-long debate over Paul's location when he wrote Philippians. We realize we're on thin ice; we always tell young pastors that if they think they've come up with an interpretation of Scripture that's brand new, they're probably wrong. We're not aware of any scholars who have argued that Paul wanted to recruit the Philippians into partnership for ministry in Spain, but we're also not aware of more than a handful of scholars who have seriously studied first-century church partnerships.

new partnerships. He wanted to see ministries multiplied, so we believe that his trip to Philippi was a partnership recruitment trip.

Beyond the Apostles

And it's exciting to know that these partnerships didn't end with Paul. Long after he and the other apostles died, churches continued to partner together—especially caring for one another when believers were in prison or suffering. In the second century, Tertullian wrote, "If there happen to be any in the mines, or banished to the islands, or shut up in the prisons, for nothing but their fidelity to the cause of God's Church," then the churches would rally together to care for them.[3]

The church fathers weren't the only ones who noticed the way Christian congregations banded together to care for the suffering among them. The pagan philosopher Lucian of Samosata wrote about his fellow philosopher Peregrinus, who was converted and later imprisoned for his faith in Syria. Lucian heard of the care that a partnership of churches brought to Peregrinus. He wrote, "Indeed, people came even from the cities in Asia, sent by Christians at their common expense, to help him with advice and consolation."[4] Did you catch that? In the second century, churches in Asia were still partnering together to care for brothers and sisters in prison in Syria. Paul's ministry of mercy had multiplied.

The Need for Multiplication

Of course, Paul was an apostle. It was his *job* to multiply ministries that would take the gospel across the Roman empire. And the early church leaders had to rely on one another because there

---

[3] Tertullian, *Apology*, 39, Loeb Classical Library, trans. T. R. Glover (Cambridge, MA: Harvard University Press, 1931), 177.
[4] Lucian, *The Passing of Peregrinus*, 12–13, Loeb Classical Library, trans. A. M. Harmon (Cambridge, MA: Harvard University Press, 1936), 13, 15. Thanks to Michael Haykin for his help with early church references.

were so few Christians at that time. Today, things are different. Most of us don't really need to find more things to do with other churches. More partnerships mean more headaches.

It's true, as we said in chapter 3, that we need to focus on the unique mission God has called us to fulfill, especially in partnership. You can't climb two mountains at the same time. But at some point, someone will have an idea for doing something different together or doing what you already do in a new place. Trust us, it always happens. At that point, you'll have a few options:

Option 1: Say Yes
Don't let any good ideas pass you by. Try to do it all. But then you run the risk that diffusing your focus will lead to confusion and exhaustion, which could eventually lead to the downfall of the partnership.

Option 2: Say No
Refuse to even consider new possibilities. Stay laser-focused on the mission to which God has called you. But then you run the risk of quenching the work of the Spirit.

Charles Spurgeon used the example of filling bottles to illustrate the pros and cons of these options. Imagine that you have placed twenty small-mouth bottles some twenty feet away from you. You have a big bucket of water to fill the bottles. You could swing the bucket in an arc from a distance of twenty feet and try to fill the bottles by throwing the water toward them. In other words, you could try to do everything at once. Or you could take the bucket to each bottle one by one, pouring in the water until it is filled, and then move to the next one. That way, you would be doing only one thing at a time, and doing it well.

We'd like to propose another option: stop pouring water and start pouring champagne. You know those giant champagne glass towers you sometimes see at weddings? As you fill the first glass, it eventually overflows and fills the ones below it, then those overflow and fill the ones below, and so on until all the glasses are full. In this way, we multiply our efforts. That's the other option to consider when ministry opportunities start flowing beyond our previously defined boundaries.

Option 3: Multiply

Consider giving birth to a new partnership. Think about what would happen if you unleashed an ever-expanding army of glass-fillers.

Ellen Livingood has seen the power of multiplication around the world: "A congregation in Canada and their long-term partners in Guatemala join in reaching a tribal village in a remote part of Guatemala. In other cases, Western churches and Majority World churches are establishing new partnerships to work together in a third country—such as Morocco, Indonesia, or Vietnam."[5] She calls such ministries 1+1=3 Partnerships.

The ultimate goal of a kingdom partnership is not simply to meet a few needs along the way. The goal is to ignite a movement!

What Makes a Movement?

Tim Keller, who has helped spark urban-ministry and church-planting movements in New York City and across the world, says there are four key characteristics of a movement: vision, sacrifice, flexibility with unity, and spontaneity.[6]

1. First and foremost, movements are marked by *a compelling vision*. A vision consists of an attractive, vivid, and clear picture of the future that the movement and its leaders are seeking to bring about. A movement states, "If this is where you want to go, come along with us." This picture of the

---

[5] Ellen Livingood, *Your Focus on the World* (Newtown, PA: Catalyst Services, 2010), 178.
[6] Timothy Keller, *Center Church: Doing Balanced, Gospel-Centered Ministry in Your City* (Grand Rapids: Zondervan, 2012), 339–40.

future is accompanied by a strong set of values or beliefs
to which the movement is committed. The content of this
vision must be expressed so that others can grasp it readily;
it must not be so esoteric or difficult that only a handful of
people can articulate it.

2. The unifying vision in a movement is so compelling that
   it leads to *a culture of sacrificial commitment and intrinsic rewards*. Individuals put the vision ahead of their own
   interests and comfort. In the early days of any movement,
   the main actors often work without compensation, constantly living in the threat of bankruptcy. The satisfaction
   of realized goals is their main reward. Some refer to this
   as "intrinsic" reward—internal, personal fulfillment that
   comes from knowing you have been instrumental in bringing about so much good.

3. Movements are characterized by *a stance of generous flexibility toward organizations and people* outside their own
   membership rolls. Movements make the accomplishment
   of the vision a higher value than how it gets done and who
   gets it done. The vision encourages sacrifice, and members
   of a movement are willing to make allies, cooperating with
   anyone who shares an interest in the vision.

4. Movements *spontaneously produce new ideas and leaders*, and therefore grow from within. By their very nature,
   institutions are structured for long-term durability and
   stability, and so are prone to resist risky ideas. But movements are willing to take risks because the members are
   already making sacrifices to be part of the work. A movement also tends to attract and reward leaders who produce
   results. Again, the reason is that accomplishing the vision
   is so important.

Some movements seem to spring up overnight. Sleepy
Christians are suddenly jolted awake, myopic churches suddenly

start ministering to their communities, and new believers suddenly start pouring into the pews. But most movements are preceded by many years of prayerful work. It takes patience to stack up a pyramid of champagne glasses, and laying the groundwork for a self-multiplying gospel movement requires the same kind of perseverance. The sudden outpouring of the Spirit in Quebec in the 1970s (see chapter 5) was preceded by decades of patient preparation. New churches, seminaries, and ministries grew and multiplied only after much soil-tilling had been done.

Ready to Reproduce?

So how do you know when you're ready to multiply and expand into new areas of ministry, or even spin off brand-new ministries? We've learned some hard lessons through our experience in the process of multiplication (or, more specifically, through our *failures* in the process of multiplication), and we've come up with a few questions to ask ourselves when we're considering something new:

Is our current ministry fully established? Are we in the "performing" stage described in chapter 5? Have we solidified our roles, systems, and best practices? Are we able to delegate responsibility and authority freely to other leaders? Are we seeing fruit in our current ministry? If we send out leaders and workers to launch this new ministry, will our current partnership still be healthy?

Have we built sufficient trust and commitment? Do we enjoy being together and working together? Do we trust one another to do what's best for the ministry and for each partner church? Do we have confidence that each partner (and especially new partners who might be coming on board for a new ministry) will follow through on their commitments?

Is there a clear need and open opportunity? Or is the proposed new ministry just something that sounds nice to do? Are there people asking for our help? Are there unbelievers who are ready to receive Christ? Are there unusual opportunities that may not last for long?

Has God provided the right catalytic leader for a new partnership? Or is the potential leader just someone who's excited about this ministry (there's a big difference)? Is he a proven, shepherd-hearted, entrepreneurial leader who can rally others around a new project? Have we evaluated this person by the four C's of leadership: character, calling, competency, capacity?

When we can answer all these questions (and others that specifically apply to different types of ministries) with a full-throated "Yes!" we know we're ready to multiply. Then it's time to hold on to our hats and glasses, because we're in for one wild ride. After all the patient and prayerful preparation, there comes a time when you've got to let go and let the wind of the Holy Spirit blow this new ministry wherever he will. That's the only way movements are unleashed.

Get Ready to Lose Control

There's one thing that often keeps ministries from multiplying into movements: our need for control. Missiologist Roland Allen noticed this tendency in the missionaries he observed:

> Many of our missionaries welcome spontaneous zeal, provided there is not too much of it for their restrictions, just as an engineer laying out the course of a river is glad of some water to fill his channels, but does not want a flood which may sweep away his embankments. Such missionaries pray for the wind of the Spirit but not for a rushing mighty wind.[7]

Allen longed to see movements spread across cities, countries, and continents, and he believed spontaneous expansion would

---

[7] Roland Allen, *The Spontaneous Expansion of the Church: And the Causes which Hinder It* (London: World Dominion Press, 1949), 17.

happen when church leaders were willing to give up some of their precious control:

> By spontaneous expansion I mean something which we *cannot* control. . . . The great things of God are beyond our control. Therein lies a vast hope. Spontaneous expansion could fill the continents with the knowledge of Christ: our control cannot reach as far as that.
>
> There is always something terrifying in the feeling that we are letting loose a force which we cannot control; and when we think of spontaneous expansion in this way, instinctively we begin to be afraid. Whether we consider our doctrine, or our civilization, or our morals, or our organization, in relation to a spontaneous expansion of the Church, we are seized with terror, terror lest spontaneous expansion should lead to disorder.[8]

Consider how a gospel movement might expand spontaneously across a city (we'll call it Metropolis):

Launching a Gospel Movement in Metropolis

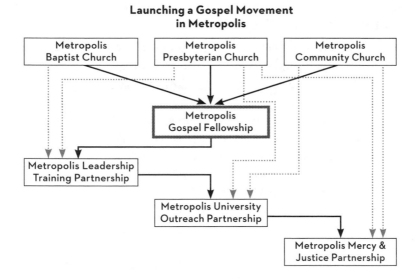

---

[8] Ibid.

Three leaders from three different churches in Metropolis might start meeting for lunch. Out of this gospel fellowship, two churches might decide to start training young leaders in theology and ministry together. One of the rising leaders in that program might sense God leading him to reach students at Metropolis University. Seeing the enormity of the task, he might rally leaders from a few other churches to join him. One of the believers on that campus might be distraught by the homeless families she sees in Metropolis Park on her way to school every morning. She might gather a few other students from different churches to start providing free tutoring and school supplies for the homeless kids in the park.

You might say that all these different partnerships have been birthed out of the gospel fellowship established by a few leaders. But that network is only the springboard, not the controlling force. Different partnerships are multiplied on their own, all involving different churches and leaders. The raging river of the Spirit starts to overflow the banks of our carefully constructed channels, and for that we praise God!

And, Lord willing, so will the people around us.

The End Goal: Glory to God and Favor from Man

When Paul spoke about the motivation behind the Jerusalem collection partnership, he said, "We carry out this act of grace that is being ministered by us, for the glory of the Lord himself. . . . We aim at what is honorable not only in the Lord's sight but also in the sight of man" (2 Cor. 8:19, 21). Paul's ultimate goal was not the expansion of his own ministry, church tribe, or theological brand. His priority was the glory of God!

Many leaders and churches enter into ministry together for many other reasons. One leader we know lamented the motivations he saw as he looked around the room at a recent meeting to discuss potential church partnership:

One pastor is only interested in being a "pastor of pastors." He only sees partnership as a ministry by him, not a ministry to him. Another couple of pastors only want to partner with those who are already part of their network and only see ministry partnerships as a way to recruit new members for a national network or denomination. Another couple of pastors want to serve the other churches, but have already determined the agenda, method, goals, and structure of the partnership. They only want partners who will get on board with what they want to do.[9]

These leaders are probably all well-meaning brothers, and we don't doubt their desire to see God's kingdom advance. But when you enter into partnership with an agenda like theirs, what happens when the needs of the partnership conflict with the needs of your church? What do you do when you find yourself facing a dilemma in partnership that you've never encountered in decades of ministry, but one that the young church planter in the urban core deals with every day? When you start with the glory of God as your motivation, your selfish ambitions and vain conceits don't get in the way of kingdom advancement.

Think about what happens when the glory of God is at the center of the movement. Believers are blessed and give thanks to God because of you: "You will be enriched in every way to be generous in every way, which through us will produce thanksgiving to God" (2 Cor. 9:11). In addition, the watching world notices "your light [shining] before others," and they "see your good works and give glory to your Father who is in heaven" (Matt. 5:16).

This is what happened when the churches of the first century turned the world upside down and when the churches of the second century caught the appreciative eye of pagan philosophers. But you may not have heard about the way this happened in the sixteenth century across the nation of France, spurred on by a catalytic leader named John Calvin.

---

[9] Comments from personal conversation.

Calvin's Geneva

If you know Calvin, you probably know him as a theologian and Bible expositor. Both of us thank God for his theological acumen and precision. Chris even gave one of his sons the middle name Calvin. Calvin's never-ending emphasis on our sovereign God gives us great encouragement, comfort, and courage in life and ministry. But what most people don't know about Calvin is that he was a passionate and prolific church planter who built a partnership for missions and church planting.[10]

In the last decade of his life, one of Calvin's highest priorities was facilitating church plants in Roman Catholic France. In 1555, Calvin had ministered in Geneva, Switzerland, for the better part of two decades. During that time, the church in Geneva, partnered with churches in Basel and Strasbourg, had planted five churches in France. With the growing persecution of Protestants in France, this was no easy task!

But those first few churches were only the beginning. From 1555 to 1559, that number expanded to one hundred. By the time Calvin died five years later, the partnership had planted more than two thousand churches in France!

And the seed multiplied in amazing ways. One planter in Montpellier wrote, "Our church, thanks to the Lord, has so grown and so continues to grow every day that we are obliged to preach three sermons on Sundays to a total of five to six thousand people."[11] Another church in Bergerac had four to five thousand. A pastor in Toulouse estimated that eight or nine thousand people gathered for worship at his church every Sunday. If these churches were in Georgia or Texas today, we'd call them megachurches. As

---

[10] Most of the information in this section is found in David McKay, "The Missionary Zeal of Calvin," a paper presented at the European Conference of Reformed Churches, Nov. 4–7, 2008, in Soest, the Netherlands. See also John Starke's summary article, "John Calvin, Missionary and Church Planter," the Gospel Coalition blog, Nov. 27, 2012, http://thegospelcoalition.org/blogs/tgc/2012/11/27/john-calvin-missionary-and-church-planter/ (accessed April 22, 2013).

[11] Cited in McKay, "The Missionary Zeal of Calvin," 4.

Calvin's church in Geneva banded together with other churches in Europe, their ministry multiplied in incredible ways.

So what was driving this fast-moving partnership? In his famous work *Institutes of the Christian Religion,* Calvin said, "Let us seek with great and ardent desire and eagerness those things which we seek only for God's glory."[12] In ministry partnership, as in theology, Calvin sought to make God's name great.

Like Calvin, let's seek to multiply our partnerships with the hope of seeing amazing growth, multiplication, and evident fruit. Let's seek to build and multiply our church partnerships with great and ardent desire and eagerness. But from beginning to end, let's seek those things only for God's glory.

Engage in kingdom partnership like Paul and Calvin did: "for the glory of the Lord himself."

Questions for Discussion:

1. When you are presented with new ideas for ministry, are you more likely to say yes or no? Why?
2. Which of the four characteristics of a movement (vision, sacrifice, flexibility with unity, and spontaneity) characterize your partnership?
3. Multiplying ministries is a delicate thing, requiring a balance of intentionality and spontaneity, strategic planning and flexibility. What are some pitfalls on each side?

---

[12] John Calvin, *Institutes of the Christian Religion,* 1536 ed., trans. Ford Lewis Battles (Grand Rapids: Eerdmans, 1995), 69.

9

Putting It All Together

Kingdom Partnership Step by Step

If you've made it this far in the book (or if you're the kind of person who starts reading a book from the back), you're probably wondering what kind of practical steps it takes to get a kingdom partnership off the ground. While we can't be exhaustive, we want to outline some steps you can take, regardless of where you're starting in partnership. Some of the suggestions we make here were put forth earlier in the book, but it is our hope that it will help you to see them collected in this step-by-step outline.

1. Overcome Your Aversion to Partnership

You're way too overwhelmed with what's already happening in your own church. You've tried working with other organizations before, but it was a mess. You can never quite see eye to eye with other churches on theology or philosophy of ministry. You're not sure you even like any other churches.

All of these objections have flitted through our minds from time to time, and you can probably think of many more. At a recent pastors' gathering in Michigan, Dan Chittock boldly confessed a few of his own reasons for failing to work with others:[1]

- *A spirit of competition.* "We can invest time and resources and people into gospel efforts in Africa, South America, or even Utah, and invariably we join hands with churches or with church planters when we do so. But joining hands with the church in the town next to me can be . . . well, threatening. We don't want to invest our time and resources and people into a project which may cause the brother across town to reap a bigger harvest."
- *A fear of results.* "What happens if these local gospel endeavors actually produce converts and those converts start coming to my church? Things can get messy! I don't mean the superficial messiness of people now attending church who smell like cigarettes, don't dress the right way and occasionally use coarse language. I mean the messiness that comes when church unity and doctrinal precision are tested."

These kinds of aversions are common to us all, but they must be overcome for the sake of the kingdom's advancement. Jesus died on the cross and rose from the dead to call us into the eternal partnership of the Trinity for a purpose much bigger than ourselves. Jesus prayed "that they may all be one, just as you, Father, are in me, and I in you, that they also may be in us, so that the world may believe that you have sent me" (John 17:21). We are brought into fellowship with the Trinity and with one another so that the world may believe and join us too!

---

[1] From the manuscript of his message.

Assessment: How open and ready is our church to partner with others?

1   2   3   4   5   6   7   8   9   10

Completely closed   –   Considering it   –   Ready and willing

_____

Planning: What aversions to partnership do we need to overcome?

2. Build Gospel Fellowship and Trust among Leaders and Churches

Regardless of the objections you or others might raise to partnership, it's never too soon to start laying the relational foundation. Every great partnership starts with gospel fellowship among like-minded leaders. And it always takes time for that to develop, usually growing through one-on-one meetings and informal gatherings. A memorandum of understanding means nothing if the relationship isn't there, so start building relationships with other leaders around you—now!

Existing relationships in a denomination or association are natural places for new partnerships to start, and they allow ministry efforts to launch quickly. But in many cases, partnerships need to expand beyond an existing association. Local pastors' prayer and networking groups can also be places for partnerships to germinate. Your partnership may need to start with just three or four pastors agreeing to meet once a month for prayer and fellowship. You never know what God might do with those relationships.

Keep in mind that rushing to get commitments too quickly can kill a budding partnership. Allow God to build the relational foundation for the ministry efforts that will come later.

Assessment: How much love and trust has been built among potential parners?

1   2   3   4   5   6   7   8   9   10

None   —   Starting to like each other   —   Band of brothers

_____

Planning: What are some practical steps we can take to build relationships?

3. Identify a Need/Opportunity and How a Partnership Could Address It

Partnerships never last long if they exist only for partnership's sake. As your fellowship grows and deepens, you'll begin to identify common ministry passions and goals. In our theological training partnership, for example, we saw the need for theologically robust, practically relevant pastoral training, so we began to brainstorm about how to meet this need. The long-term result has been a church-based pastoral training program, but it did not start overnight. We spent several years praying, brainstorming, planning, and fund-raising before we launched. Your partnerships will be no different. So as you move through the early stages of praying about partnerships, remember the three essential ingredients to consider: *need*, *opportunity*, and *congruity*:

- *Is there a need?* Are there people in physical or emotional need who could be served effectively by a group of churches? Is there a crisis you could respond to with long-term ministry? Are there underreached geographical areas, people groups, or segments of the culture where the gospel has not yet penetrated effectively? Are there places where more churches should be planted? Are there leaders who are not being sufficiently equipped?

- *Is there an opportunity?* Are there people who are asking for practical help? Are there unbelievers who are ready to receive Christ? Are there churches or believers who are asking for training and expertise? Are there unusual opportunities that may not last for long?
- *Is there congruity?* Are there other leaders and churches who share the same burden as you to meet the need you've identified? Are they willing to invest time, energy, and resources? Do they have a strong passion for this ministry, or could it be that you're dragging them into partnership by sheer force of personality and persuasion?

Answering these questions up front will help you avoid wasting time and resources along the way pursuing projects and partners toward which God is not actually calling you.

Assessment: Do we have a clearly identified need/ opportunity, and a unified desire to address it?

1	2	3	4	5	6	7	8	9	10

Not a clue   —   Still assessing   —   Locked and loaded

Planning: What kind of need/opportunity will we address together?

---

4. Build the Partnership on a Foundation of Prayer

This can easily become a perfunctory step for fast-moving leaders who are tempted to act first and pray later. But a partnership that's driven by the gospel is naturally drawn toward serious prayer, since leaders come with the realization that they are desperately dependent on God's power and grace for everything. Prayer is not an agenda item, it is the lifeblood of the ministry.

John Piper explains:

> Is it true that intentional, regular, disciplined, earnest, Christ-dependent, God-glorifying, joyful prayer is a duty? You can call it that. It's a duty the way it's the duty of a scuba diver to put on his air tank before he goes underwater. It's a duty the way pilots listen to air traffic controllers. It's a duty the way soldiers in combat clean their rifles and load their guns. It's a duty the way hungry people eat food. It's a duty the way thirsty people drink water. It's a duty the way a deaf man puts in his hearing aid. It's a duty the way a diabetic takes his insulin. It's a duty the way Pooh Bear looks for honey. It's a duty the way pirates look for gold.[2]

God urges us toward this kind of joyful dependence in our efforts to advance his kingdom: "You who put the LORD in remembrance, take no rest, and *give him no rest* until he establishes Jerusalem and makes it a praise in the earth" (Isa. 62:6–7). Incredible! You probably couldn't get a meeting with the mayor of your city, but the Creator of the universe invites you to come straight to him and keep nagging him until he acts.

Assessment: Do we honestly and consistently sense our desperate dependence on God in prayer for this ministry?

1	2	3	4	5	6	7	8	9	10

No, we've got this   —   Maybe he could help   —   SOS!

Planning: How can we discipline ourselves to pray more often and more seriously?

---

[2] John Piper, "Put in the Fire for the Sake of Prayer," sermon delivered Dec. 28, 2008, www.desiringgod.org/resource-library/sermons/put-in-the-fire-for-the-sake-of-prayer (accessed Aug. 5, 2012).

5. Look for Similar Efforts You Can Imitate

Don't try to reinvent the wheel. There is probably some other church, partnership, or nonprofit organization somewhere in the world that's doing what you want to do. Contact the partners and learn from their successes and failures. Get everything they have in writing and copy what you can from their systems and procedures. You'll need to customize everything for your own context, but it's a lot easier to edit than it is to create.

When we established a theological training program, we found a few other partnerships around the world that were doing the same thing. We spent hours on Skype with leaders in these churches and we asked for all the paperwork they could send. Of course, we're doing things differently than anyone else, but we avoided quite a few pitfalls by taking the time to ask and learn.

Assessment: How proactive have we been to learn from others?

1   2   3   4   5   6   7   8   9   10

We're loners   —   We can learn a few things   —   Help!

Planning: Which churches, parachurch organizations, or charities can we approach to learn about this type of ministry?

---

6. Get Commitments from Individual Partners

Eventually, everyone needs to understand what they're expected to do. A healthy partnership is made up of partners with clear identities and roles in the mission. This helps build ownership and responsibility. Remember these principles as you elicit commitments from partners:

- *Avoid an atmosphere of pressure and guilt.* Leaders and churches that feel guilt-tripped into giving may give only what it takes to burnish their image and get you off their backs. Instead, like Paul, we want to inspire unsparing generosity.
- *Cultivate an atmosphere of delight in duty.* Duty and delight don't need to be in conflict. We should love doing what we ought to do.
- *Cultivate an atmosphere of mutual praise.* Let other leaders and churches run with ideas and initiatives that might not be particularly exciting to you, but that still contribute to the overall mission of the partnership. Kill your pride, and don't be surprised when the idea that you thought would never work turns out to be just the thing your ministry needed.
- *Cultivate an atmosphere of openness and accountability.* For leaders and churches to be true shepherds rather than hired hands, they need to understand they are investing resources, people, and sweat in a coequal partnership, not just giving to a faceless institution or a celebrity leader.

Another way to build ownership is to make sure there's an "owner" for every aspect or function of the ministry. When everyone owns everything, then no one owns anything, and everything gets neglected.

Assessment: Do partners feel a sense of ownership for specific commitments?

        1   2   3   4   5   6   7   8   9   10

Like a lazy fast-food employee   —   Like a workaholic entrepreneur

---

Planning: What commitments do we need partners to make? What are some practical ways we could help each other gain motivation and ownership?

7. Agree on a Facilitator and Leadership Structure, and Establish the Decision-Making Process

You need someone to keep leading the charge. This isn't always the catalyst who brought everyone together and got you pointed in the same direction. Those kinds of fire-breathing entrepreneurs aren't usually wired for the long-term work of nurturing relationships and managing ministries. Brash and outspoken Peter was clearly the catalytic leader of the Jerusalem church on the day of Pentecost (Acts 2), but then James rose to leadership when the church needed a bridge-builder who would maintain unity in mission as they faced contentious issues that could easily split them apart (Acts 15). Consider the four C's of leadership when deciding on a facilitator: character, calling, competency, and capacity.

The facilitator's job is inherently a lonely one, so look for ways to form a leadership team that will help him shoulder the burden. There are many ways to structure it, from an executive director and board to a plurality of coequal leaders. To foster a sense of ownership and an atmosphere of openness, it's ideal to have a leader from each church who helps guide the partnership. Just make sure the question of structure doesn't overshadow the mission that brought you together.

As a partnership grows, the leadership structure needs to change. Large teams tend to lose independent insights and just start agreeing with one another. That's why Amazon.com founder Jeff Bezos uses the "two-pizza rule" as he chooses the size of his teams: if a team can't be fed by two pizzas alone, that team is too large.[3] So for partnerships that are growing past seven churches or so, we recommend establishing a small "executive" leadership team that meets every one to two months to oversee the day-to-day operations, along with an "advisory" team with members from every church that meets every three to six months to provide ongoing input.

[3] Adam Dachis, "Follow Jeff Bezos' Two Pizza Rule to Avoid the Dangers of 'Groupthink,'" Dec. 3, 2012, http://lifehacker.com/5965280/follow-jeff-bezos-two-pizza-rule-to-avoid-the-dangers-of-groupthink (accessed Feb. 21, 2014).

As you establish the structure and decision-making process, it's also crucial to establish an exit strategy. Make sure you have an answer for this all-important question: "How will we know when this partnership is no longer fruitful, effective, or healthy?"

Assessment: Do we have a structure in place for decision-making and delegation?

1   2   3   4   5   6   7   8   9   10

We'd rather wing it   —   We've talked about it   —   It's in ink

_____

Planning: What kind of structure would best serve our unique partnership, location, cultural context, etc.?

---

8. Launch the Ministry

Eventually, you need to "just do it." While prayer and careful planning are necessary, launching a church partnership is a lot like getting married: if you wait until everything's perfect to pull the trigger, it'll never happen. Expect to learn as you go and be ready to do some plane-building while you're flying.

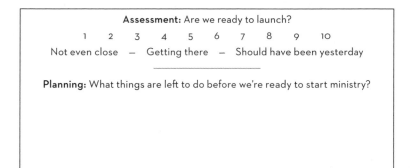

Assessment: Are we ready to launch?

1   2   3   4   5   6   7   8   9   10

Not even close   —   Getting there   —   Should have been yesterday

_____

Planning: What things are left to do before we're ready to start ministry?

9. Meet Regularly to Pray, Evaluate, and Plan

Once the plane is airborne, it's tempting to put it on autopilot, assuming that as long as each church is fulfilling its commitment, there's no need to fill our schedules with more meetings. Don't give in to that temptation. Regular meetings are necessary to maintain relationships of trust and to spot potential problems before they become dangerous.

For partnerships in a single city or region, planning meetings are easier. For partnerships that span countries and continents, they require some creativity. Find ways to utilize technology so you can communicate regularly, but make a point to meet face to face too. No matter how good the resolution is on your webcam, it can't convey your heart very well.

Don't neglect regular evaluation. You will be tempted to overlook failures of strategy and leadership in order to preserve unity. Don't fall for it. Healthy partnerships are open and transparent about everything, which inevitably leads to some confrontation and conflict.

Assessment: Do we meet regularly to pray, evaluate, and plan?

1 2 3 4 5 6 7 8 9 10

E-mailed last year — Phoned last month — Met last week

Planning: How will we ensure that we're regularly communicating, praying, and assessing our progress together?

---

10. Celebrate God's Grace

Every time the leadership team meets, take time to share together and praise God for all the evidences of his grace in the partnership. Send out newsletters and create videos that partner churches can use to inspire their whole congregations to celebrate as well. Praise one another publicly and regularly. Jesus is our Advocate before the Father, continually speaking the best of each one of us—how could we do any different for one another?

In his book *Practicing Affirmation*, Sam Crabtree challenges us to get specific in our praise:

> I am not primarily interested in generic, vanilla, fuzzy, imprecise, and dubious compliments with approval of something vague. Get specific. "Nice job"—what exactly was nice about it? "Gnarly, dude"—what aspects were so gnarly? I'm often guilty of this next one: "Remarkable"—just what is it that is so remarkable? Remark about it! I desire for us to see and affirm the work of God in persons as evidenced by sightings of the character of his well-pleasing Son manifest in them.[4]

Assessment: How well do we celebrate the work of God in our partnership and in each other?

1	2	3	4	5	6	7	8	9	10

That's Jesus's job — Every once in a while — All the time

_____

Planning: What are some creative ways we can communicate what God is doing through this partnership to our churches and others?

---

11. Be Patient and Flexible

Things Fall Apart is the title of a novel about how groups and cultures continually change, and how those that don't adapt

---

[4]Sam Crabtree, *Practicing Affirmation: God-Centered Praise of Those Who Are Not God* (Wheaton: Crossway, 2011), 134.

eventually die. The same is true of partnerships. They take a long time to develop, and they must constantly shift in response to new opportunities, needs, and partners. Maintaining a partnership is much harder than starting it, so be patient!

Remember the typical progression of any cooperative ministry (from chapter 5):

- *Forming.* Passionately uniting around a common identity and mission, but not accomplishing much yet.
- *Storming.* Starting to accomplish things, but experiencing confusion, conflict, and lack of commitment.
- *Norming.* Creating structures and systems, often deferring to others to maintain momentum.
- *Performing.* Delegating responsibility and authority as we experience maximum ministry effectiveness.

Expect to revisit some of those stages when people, situations, or needs change. Even if you're a young-earth creationist, don't be afraid to evolve a little bit.

Assessment: How flexible are we in carrying out this ministry?

1   2   3   4   5   6   7   8   9   10

Absolutely unbendable   —   Somewhat malleable   —   Gumby

_____

Planning: Where is our partnership in the four stages of cooperative ministry above? What should we do to reach the next stage?

---

12. Consolidate

After the initial excitement fades, some partners realize this ministry just isn't for them (or at least not for this season), and they choose not to continue. It's always disappointing, but always to be expected. As Charles Spurgeon said:

> Be not surprised when friends fail you: it is a failing world. Never count upon immutability in man: inconstancy you may reckon upon without fear of disappointment. The disciples of Jesus forsook him; be not amazed if your adherents wander away . . . as they were not your all when with you, all is not gone from you with their departure.[5]

Some wishy-washiness is to be expected. Just don't let partners sit on the fence for too long. It's important to know who's in and who's out so you know what to expect from them. Release exiting partners with humility, love, and blessing.

Assessment: Have we clearly established who's in and who's out?

1   2   3   4   5   6   7   8   9   10

We don't want to pressure anyone   —   We've taken people off our website

_____

Planning: How can we encourage wishy-washy partners to commit more strongly? Are there any we should release with our blessing?

---

13. Relaunch

All partnerships must be tweaked along the way. Most times this can be done gradually and quietly, but sometimes the whole partnership needs a "relaunch" one or two years down the road. Use it as an opportunity to refine your goals and strategy, refresh your expectations for one another, and reestablish your depen-

---

[5] Charles Haddon Spurgeon, "The Minister's Fainting Fits," in *Lectures to My Students* (Grand Rapids: Zondervan, 1979), 164.

dence on God for it all. You might need to consider a relaunch if (1) you've come to see that your original goals are unattainable; (2) your current strategies for achieving your goals aren't working; or (3) partner enthusiasm is waning.

Assessment: Is it time for us to relaunch?

    1   2   3   4   5   6   7   8   9   10
No, we're doing great — It's possible — Hit the reset button!

_____

Planning: If we're currently struggling, how would a relaunch affect our partnership? Could it bring back focus, commitment, and enthusiasm?

---

14. Multiply

All healthy things grow and reproduce, and healthy partnerships are no exception. Be ready to spin off partnerships that will address new opportunities and needs. Remember to ask yourselves these questions to know when you're ready to multiply:

- *Is our current ministry fully established?* Are we seeing fruit in our current ministry? If we send out some leaders and workers to launch this new ministry, will our current partnership still be healthy?
- *Have we built sufficient trust and commitment?* Do we enjoy being together and working together? Do we trust one another to do what's best for the ministry and for each partner church?
- *Is there a clear need and open opportunity?* Or is it just something that sounds nice to do? Are there people asking for our help?

- *Has God provided the right catalytic leader for a new partnership?* Is he a proven entrepreneurial leader who can rally others around a new project?

Assessment: Are we ready to multiply yet?

1	2	3	4	5	6	7	8	9	10

Not even close   —   Maybe in a year   —   Ready to reproduce

---

Planning: What kind of ministry do we believe God might be calling us to pursue that doesn't match our current mission? How might we send out leaders and workers in partnership to address this opportunity?

Remember, It's God's Work

"Unless the LORD builds the house, those who build it labor in vain" (Ps. 127:1).

As you work to build your kingdom partnership, remember that it is just like every other ministry that God has called you to lead. You will hit roadblocks, forks in the road, and plenty of discouragement. But don't forget step #4—keep on praying. Remember that this is ultimately God's work, and he will build it. None of these steps will matter unless God is in it, and we can have confidence that when we are seeking his glory in our partnerships, he will build them.

Appendix

Frequently Asked Questions

Isn't it better to let the experts do it?

Whether you want to train leaders, care for the poor, or plant churches, there are always larger and more experienced organizations out there that could do it for you. By all means, we should glean from the experts, but we shouldn't outsource our God-given responsibility to them. For example, while we believe that we should take advantage of seminaries' in-depth scholarship and resources, we should do so without relinquishing our responsibility and authority to train pastors within the local church. The key question is whether an organization does ministry *with* your church or *instead* of your church.

What is the difference between a local church, a parachurch ministry, and a kingdom partnership?

A local church is a single congregation with distinct leadership, membership, and ministries under the oversight of its elders and other members. A parachurch ministry is not a church, but rather an organization that comes alongside and assists the church in her mission. Typically, a parachurch ministry has a more focused purpose, such as a sports ministry or providing food for the homeless. But a church partnership is a shared ministry of one or more local churches. Unlike most parachurch ministries, it is still very much under the direct supervision of the local church. However, unlike the ministry of a single local church, partnerships belong equally to the partner churches.

So are all parachurch organizations bad?

Not at all! A partnership could be considered a parachurch organization. Any organization whose goal is to support the ministry of local churches can be great! When Jay Jarman was distressed by an epidemic of lonely, ignored, at-risk kids (see chapter 7), he could have built an independent organization and recruited mentors out of churches to join him. Instead, he decided to focus on training mentors within their local churches and helping each church establish its own partnership with a local school. Common Grace is an example of a partnership (or a parachurch organization) that's enhancing the ministry of the local church, not replacing it.

I believe God is calling our church toward a particular kingdom partnership, but our senior pastor isn't very interested. What should I do?

Be patient and pray. Connect him with people who would be helped by your partnership. Just be careful not to manipulate his emotions or have him do ministry that is not helpful for anything other than grabbing his heart. In overseas countries, we've seen missions organizations plan seminars for local church leaders that involved bringing in senior pastors from large and wealthy American churches to speak. The local leaders rarely learn anything new from these one-shot trainings—they are simply used as props to tug at the heartstrings and purse strings of the American pastors.

Don't settle for tacit approval from the leadership of your church, then go off and do your own thing. Ellen Livingood challenges pastors to recognize that if God is leading your congregation to partnership, "it requires your heartfelt ownership. Ownership does not mean you accept responsibility for administration or implementation. However, it is crucial that you incorporate the [partnership's] vision and goals into your preaching, weigh these priorities into all your decision making, and emphasize by word and deed your personal commitment."[1]

What should we do if churches that don't agree with our doctrinal statement want to join our partnership?

If God gives your partnership some level of apparent success, you will attract more churches. Sometimes those churches won't be on the same theological page as you. All partnerships need to decide early which doctrinal issues are essential and which are secondary and can be set aside when it comes to the partnership.

If you are partnering together in a crisis pregnancy center, your soteriology probably won't matter too much beyond a shared belief in salvation by grace through faith. But if you are partnering to train pastors, the differences between Calvinism and Arminianism could be a sticking point. Make sure your theological cards are on the table at the very beginning so that no one joins a partnership only to discover later that he disagrees with a key doctrinal distinctive.

This all sounds great, but who's going to pay for it?

You are! Without a financial commitment from the partner churches, it's hard to get a kingdom partnership off the ground. While each member of a partnership contributes different things (some more money, others more volunteers, etc.), it helps for each partner to have some skin in the game.

---

[1] Ellen Livingood, *Your Focus on the World* (Newtown, PA: Catalyst Services, 2010), 205.

Even a small, newly planted church can commit $100 each month toward a ministry partnership it believes in.

As the needs become clear and the goals of the partnership crystallize, partner churches should see that a ministry worth doing is a ministry worth paying for. While outside resources might be necessary at times, if you've learned anything from the Jerusalem collection partnership, it should be that kingdom partnerships require financial sacrifice.

When should a partnership end?

It depends on the goal of the partnership. The Jerusalem collection partnership effectively ended when their delegates delivered the gift to the Jerusalem church along with Paul. But that doesn't mean the collaboration of the Mediterranean churches ended. In fact, many of the representatives at the Council of Nicea in AD 325 came from the same churches that were involved in the collection partnership three centuries earlier.

According to missions strategist Monroe Brewer, there are three good reasons for a partnership to end: (1) you've reached your goal, (2) the project is too big or complicated, or (3) it's urged by all. There are also three bad reasons to end a partnership: (1) it was only the "pet" of one partner, (2) you're expecting results too quickly, or (3) you're discouraged.[2]

If a partnership must die, whether for good or bad reasons, look for ways God might resurrect it in a different form for a different purpose.

---

[2] Monroe Brewer, materials published by Centers of Church Based Training.

General Index

Twin Cities Church, 81–82
"two-pizza rule," 153

United Student Christian Council,
   47
unity, 19–20, 28–29, 61–62
University Christian Movement,
   47–48
unsparingness, 120–21
urgency, 118–19
uselessness, 108–9

vision, 136–37
Vonnegut, Kurt, 50–51

Waikiki, 30
Wellington, Wilfred, 84
Wilder, Robert P., 47n17
wisdom, 56
Wood, Tom, 52n2
worship, 33

YMCA, 47

Scripture Index